Climbing Through Storms:

Managing Adversity in a VUCA World

By Jeff B. Evans, PA-C

Published by MountainVision Publishing

June 2020

Printed and bound in the United States of America.

Cover photo by Didrik Johnck

ISBN: 978-1-7351140-1-9 (KDP)

ISBN: 978-1-7351140-0-2 (Ingram Spark)

Visit the author's website at www.jeffbevans.com for information about speaking event opportunities and/or obtaining signed copies of this book. To inquire about volume discounts and special requirements, contact the publisher at info@mountain-vision.com

**To all who seek out adventure
and find meaning within it.**

The world is full of motivational authors and speakers; however, very few have lived a life who not only talk the talk, but walk the walk as well. Whether by intent, happenstance, some great divine plan, or a combination of all the above, Jeff Evans has spent a life defined by VUCA situations. In Climbing Through Storms, Jeff provides his insight on how living a life on the edge of chaos, engulfed in adversity, and continuous change can define an individual. It doesn't matter if you're a seasoned adventurer or someone in need of inspiration to change your life—Jeff never fails to deliver.

JOHNNIE L GILPEN, JR PA-C NRP
USN (ret) Fleet Marine Force corpsman
2017 Pat Tillman Foundation Tillman Scholar
2019 War Horse Journal Writing Fellow

Leading in the military, business, or life when things are going smooth and well is easy; anyone can do it. It's not until crisis strikes with paralyzing stress, the "fog of war" and high-stakes consequences surrounding the situation do you find truly great leadership with unshakeable composure and decisiveness. Having been fortunate to spend a career in orbit of some of history's greatest military leaders collectively immersed in VUCA situations, Jeff sits among the top of my list of great leaders. A most captivating articulation of the applied principles of leadership in volatile, uncertain, complex, and ambiguous situations—required reading for VUCA leaders.

LCDR MARK 'OZ' OZDARSKI, USN (RET)
SEAL Team 6

I have spent the better part of my entire adulthood adventuring all over the world with Jeff and have shared many of the experiences he reflects on in this book. I have been witness to Jeff managing countless VUCA type situations in a real time, real consequence theater, and I am grateful for every moment of it. Sit back and enjoy the stories and lessons that come from a VUCA life well lived.

ERIK WEIHENMAYER
First blind man to summit Mount Everest

I have spent the majority of my life working in chaotic and complex scenarios. From my career as a Tier One Special Forces operator as well as summiting the fourteen highest mountains in the world in six months, I have been required to manage VUCA landscapes at a very high level. Climbing Through Storms *wonderfully encapsulates all the strategies and theories that have proven to be personally valuable to me in both of my professional worlds as well as being a husband and family man in civilian life. Kudos to Jeff for bringing together such a meaningful collection of stories and lessons.*

NIRMAL PURJA MBE — "NIMS"
Former UK Special Forces
14 x 8,000 meter peaks in six months
10x Guinness Record Holder on 8,000-meter peaks

Acknowledgments

I have leaned on a lot of folks to bring this book out of my head and onto paper. It sprang forth from the ether one day standing in waist-deep water on a remote Mexican beach with my wife, Merry Beth, waiting for the wind to pick up so we could kitesurf. Just a few weeks prior, I had appeared as a guest on *The Joe Rogan Experience* podcast (Episode 977) and was continuing to field daily messages from folks who were intrigued by my story, one of them being a book-publishing agent. He suggested I capture my stories and distill out the VUCA message. MB and I stood in the water that day and sketched the outline and broad learning points. Fast-forward two years, and we have ourselves a book.

I am grateful to the teammates, friends, and communities I shared these powerful life experiences with. Each of them contributed to my welfare and provided me with vast opportunities to learn.

I owe my life to the many climbing partners I have roped up with over the years, and whom I have unconditionally trusted.

More thanks to Erik Weihenmayer, who, in his blindness, has provided me sight. Being his brother and guide has required me to open my eyes wider, taking in the world around me in a more profound way.

And a heap of gratitude to my "beta-reader" team of extraordinary friends and family including, Ria Mullins, Johnny Gilpin, Skyler Williams, my brother Chris, my wife MB, and my parents Bob and Peggy. They all spent countless hours correcting my crappy grammar, moderating my folksy writing style, and making worthy suggestions. I am thankful to all of them for the time and effort, and for their love.

And for my son, Jace, who will always be my greatest source of love and adoration, and who has now become my favorite adventure partner.

Most importantly thanks to my best friend and wife, Merry Beth...who makes all things happen. Without her, I am capable of very little.

Table of Contents

About the Author

Foreword by Erik Weihenmayer

My life seems to be one challenging moment, followed by the next and then the next. As a blind man, I have learned to accept the fact that I am going to confront more volatile, uncertain, chaotic, and ambiguous situations than a sighted person. What I also learned early on is that in order to effectively walk through these perplexing scenarios, I would need to align with individuals who had an uncanny knack for calmly dealing when these things are sideways.

Jeff is one of those people.

In our quarter century of gallivanting around the globe together, Jeff and I have gotten ourselves into a whole heap of complex situations... some of which were fun, some...not so much. What's always universal in those moments is how as a team we handle adversity because, whether we like it or not, the train comes off the tracks frequently.

Not being able to see requires me to always "look" to my teammates to gain a sense of how dire things really are. If my teammates are freaking out, I start freaking out, and generally, that never ends well. I always lean toward teammates who are calm under pressure and handle adversity with a sense of humor, grit, and candor.

Jeff is the adventure partner who I have been with the longest, and there is a reason for that. He understands some fundamental truths about volatile environments. He knows that they are inevitable. He is capable of not only handling himself when things are chaotic, but doubling down and guiding me through the storm as well. It takes a special and talented person to strike that balance. Jeff does it with wit, transparency, and insightfulness. I attribute much of that to the fact that Jeff truly understands how to operate in volatility, uncertainty, complexity, and ambiguity (VUCA) environments at a very high level.

In this book, chock full of anecdotal stories from Jeff's life, you will discover the methods he has gleaned while charging into complexity... many of which were learned from decades of working with *me*.

Sit back and enjoy a life well lived in some of the most VUCA environments you can imagine.

ERIK WEIHENMAYER
Blind Adventurer
First blind man to summit Mount Everest

Prologue

"It is not the strongest species that survive, nor the most intelligent, but the ones who are the most responsive to change."
— Chuck Darwin

I was around four years old when a show called *Emergency* hit the television airwaves. This awesome series documenting the lives of Los Angeles County Fire Department paramedics was full of cool dudes doing cool medical shit. Decades before Clooney was on *ER* or *Grey's Anatomy* was my wife's favorite show, *Emergency* followed Roy Desoto and John Gage all over Los Angeles in their old school fire truck, saving lives and the occasional cat out of a tree.

At such an impressionable age, I was hooked, and they were my heroes. For my fourth birthday, I asked for and received a youth medical kit complete with a thermometer, stethoscope, and pretend syringe. My folks love to tell the story of me walking around with my kit and asking anyone within eyeshot to "roll ovah…I need to take your pertemperturp." I toted that med kit everywhere I went with that little plastic stethoscope around my neck, seeking out potential patients and scenarios to be of service.

Clearly, at a very early age, I was fascinated with the concept of helping folks who are in grave need in the middle of figurative and literal storms. Little did I know how far into the deep end I would take it.

At the ripe age of nineteen, I cut the umbilical cord, packed up my truck, and was that "headed west young man" and landed in the wilds of Colorado, where I quickly found that rock and mountain climbing was abundant and satisfied my burgeoning desire to explore, push, and suffer. I found deep satisfaction on the sides of rocks and flanks of mountains alongside friends and partners, developing relationships that were forged through long days of joy, exhaustion, and occasionally, fear. These days would be my first foray into the next level of managing complex environments.

Then, somewhere along the way, it occurred to me that I wasn't that smart. It was pointed out rather clearly over my first full summer in Colorado that I really wasn't that bright. True story. Perhaps I had developed some common-sense smarts from being a climbing bum living out of my van, but I was far from academic smart. That much became clear when I started dating a gal who was living in Boulder on her summer break from Brown University. I was fascinated with how smart she was, and there was a clear disparity with intellect when the two of us talked about any given topic. I was absolutely out of my league. As soon as she got back to Brown and all those coequal smart folks that fall, she promptly dumped me. I'll always be grateful to her for asking me to do a self-inventory on who I wanted to be and how hard was I willing to work for it.

Medicine still seemed like a solid pursuit, maybe an EMT or paramedic, but that would require me to go to school and get smart. The self-doubt crept in. I was acutely aware that I was neither disciplined nor smart enough to pursue a university degree. But as timing would have it, the week I was seriously percolating on my shortcomings and weighing the idea of trying my hand at higher education vs. sticking with the life of a mountain guide, a close friend fell off Longs Peak to his death, leaving his newlywed wife a widow. His death pushed me into a bit of a spiral as I was trying to justify a full-time career that was clearly dangerous. He was a far superior climber than I was, and his one wrong step took him from this Earth. Surely the same could happen to me. The philosophical questioning became all consuming: the more fulfilling and exciting path of climbing full time would also be fraught with danger (pretty much what I was looking for at the time) saddled up against a more conventional career path of medicine. One thing I was fairly certain of, I wanted a family one day and, by default, needed to construct a future that had a bit more security. That in itself was a driving force in my career decision-making. All of us, at some point, have to make calls that balance the notion of staying safe in the harbor or cutting the bowlines and heading out into a stormy sea. It's that equilibrium that proves to be massively subjective and ultimately helps to define the tapestry of each of our lives.

So why couldn't I have both? This epiphany would set the direction of my life in motion. Why not forge out a career that marries the two loves of my life: medicine and mountains. Get my undergrad degree and pursue a medical career, and, all the while, climb for fun, and occasionally for money.

It made sense. The job security and relative safety of a traditional career synced up with climbing would scratch both of my itches. Another bonus with this hybrid pursuit was clear—these rugged places that brought me so much joy were also filled with danger and potential injury. If my intention was to spend a large number of my days out charging in the hills with friends, I best be prepared to take care of folks when the proverbial wheels fall off the wagon.

Once I set my mind off in this trajectory, I connected the dots from my undergraduate degree at the University of Colorado in Boulder to taking a wilderness EMT course all the way up to graduating from a physician assistant program with an emphasis in emergency medicine. During all of this training and education, I continued to find ways to play in the big mountains with an attempt to keep my climbing game strong, so I would still be on point following graduation.

As the two combined skill sets of medicine and climbing began to congeal, I found myself a reasonably hot commodity on the expeditionary climbing circuit. I began receiving a glut of invitations to join large-scale climbing expeditions as the "team doc." As a green, new grad, emergency room physician assistant (PA), it was often painful to decline these offers in an effort to hold down the cherished ER job. But the adventure pull was too strong from time to time, and I found myself subscribing to the Joseph Campbell philosophy of following my bliss with complete disregard for conventional constructs like jobs and 401k plans (okay, that might be my personal slant on Campbell's *Hero's Journey* message). After only a year in the emergency department, I quit my job and joined my blind buddy, Erik, for an attempt on Mount Everest. Talk about cutting the bowlines. I shredded them.

And as they say, the rest is history…much of which you will find in this book.

I have been extremely blessed to manufacture a way to blend two careers into one. A curious byproduct of this amalgam has been finding myself seemingly always in the middle of fairly intense situations.

Sometimes I love it.

Sometimes I don't.

Oftentimes I find myself saying out loud, "Here we go again," and occasionally making blank promises to the Great Spirit above that if I get out of this mess, I promise to never do it again. Those void agreements typically last for a month or two only to be broken as the next mission calls.

Over the decades of finding myself in these situations, I have finally asked myself a few pointed questions:

Why do I actively seek out these environments?

- Is it for the adrenaline surge?
- Is it to show off in some way? Prove myself to the world, maybe.
- Is it to challenge myself and discover my abilities and limitations?
- Do I think I'm particularly good at dealing with chaos?

And more importantly, since I do regularly find myself in these storms, what skills do I need to hone to be the best version of me that I can be in those situations?

These inventory queries generate slightly different answers in every situation, project, or objective. But my curiosity on the matter has been piqued, and the result of that is this book. I felt compelled to explore the concepts of how and why chaotic environments permeate our lives and how to perform better when placed in the middle of it all.

Although we all have chaos in our lives, I tend to seek it out—for better or for worse. I figured I owed it to myself to attempt to understand how I can better perform when I voluntarily enter into these volatile, uncertain, chaotic, and ambiguous environments. We all owe it to ourselves and the people around us to take a deeper dive into how we handle adverse situations in an attempt to be a better individual, parent, spouse, employee, boss, or teammate.

These are the topics within this book that I plan to ruminate on based on many of the life experiences I have had.

Chapter 1: Life in a VUCA World

"Chaos is what we've lost touch with. This is why it is given a bad name. It is feared by the dominant archetype of our world, which is Ego, which clenches because its existence is defined in terms of control."

— **Terence McKenna**

The poo is gonna hit the fan. It's inevitable, frequent, life changing, and character defining. Things go sideways all of the time. It may be as simple as a flight being canceled and not being able to get home for dinner or as paradigm shifting as receiving a Stage IV lung cancer diagnosis at the age of forty-five. Life is full of chaos, change, and adversity.

Every day that passes for each of us, we broaden our scope of understanding how adversity and chaos can provide us an unadulterated butt whoopin'. By the time we reach middle age, our adversity calluses have developed, and we are more capable of dealing with the occasional bad hand.

But sometimes we hold back because we are afraid of the uncertainty. We are fearful that we won't be able to handle the potential failure. And isn't it true that at some point, each of us has been guilty of not embarking on a mission or an undertaking simply because we were afraid of the guaranteed chaos that would accompany the task? This fear is somehow a part of our genetic wiring for self-preservation. Undoubtedly, some of us can manage it better than others, and, in fact, some of us actually thrive in challenging environments.

For as long as I can remember, I have been endlessly enamored with the complexity and elaborateness of the world that surrounds me. As a young boy growing up in the Blue Ridge Mountains, I yearned to scamper around the woods and hills, uncovering logs, climbing trees, and looking for arrowheads. It became clear that my being front and center as the natural world shook out before me was the only activity that could quell my youthful restlessness. As I grew and expanded my playground, I continued to find that the mountains, oceans, and deserts—the wild places—made the most sense to me. It felt as though the wilderness was the perfect theater where chaos and order danced in synchronized harmony. It was this curiosity and thirst for natural chaos and order that burgeoned into a life of adventure.

Even in my early twenties, I was taking note of the fact that rock climbing provided an opportunity to place myself in a realm where chaos and order had to be managed effectively, or there would be significant consequences, i.e., long, painful falls. I found myself fascinated with the delicate balance that it took to move my body up the rock, oftentimes precariously hanging on the lip of a rock face, trying to solve the mystery maze of moves that lay above me. It was this puzzle of uncertainty that captivated me and established a hunger for intense experiences that required focus, clarity, intent, and engagement.

But a nuance began to surface as I followed my main passions of medicine and climbing. I continuously found myself craving complex situations that most folks found overwhelming and scary. The experiences that I would have in these situations would require the absolute best version of me that, I found from time to time, is simply not accessible. So my curiosity and need to understand how I can best perform when things are at their worst became somewhat of a hobby for me.

These feelings were never stronger than when I returned from my volunteer stint in Mosul (See Chapter 2). I found myself understandably struggling with many of the actions and events that had taken place there. Thankfully, I was able to tap into my network of military friends, specifically special operators and combat medics. These men spoke from experience and a shared appreciation for how some of us seem to regularly find ourselves "down range," which essentially means "deep in the shit."

It was one of these men, a fifteen-year SEAL Team 6 veteran who introduced me to an acronym that would deeply resonate with me and provide a rallying point where I could assemble the skills and intentions necessary for me to continue working in these extreme environments.

V(Volatile), **U**(Uncertain), **C**(Complex), **A**(Ambiguous)

The acronym VUCA was created by faculty members from the U.S. Army War College sometime in the mid-eighties with the intention of outfitting their up-and-coming graduates with the tools necessary to operate in the ever-changing theater of war. One could speculate that combat is undoubtedly the most chaotic environment in which a human being can maneuver. I can also surmise that victory on the battlefield is typically awarded to those who maintain a calculated presence in the face of the frenzy and fear. The War College was keenly aware of this concept and set out to teach their students the nuances of situational awareness when things unraveled in the heat of combat. But the stark reality is, although most of us are not operating in a combat theater, we all still encounter and operate in challenging professional and personal environments on a daily basis. Once you define and contemporize each of the VUCA descriptors as it was presented by the War College in literal terms, it becomes quite relatable, no matter what your role.

Volatility: We live in a world that's constantly changing, becoming more unstable each day, where changes big and small are becoming more unpredictable—and they're getting more and more dramatic and happening faster and faster. As events unfold in completely unexpected ways, it's becoming impossible to determine cause and effect.

Uncertainty: It's becoming more difficult to anticipate events or predict how they'll unfold; historical forecasts and past experiences are losing their relevance and are rarely applicable as a basis for predicting the shape of things to come. In many cases, it may be impossible to prepare for adverse situations, much less develop a plan for action, development, and growth as it is becoming increasingly uncertain where the route is heading.

Complexity: Our modern world is more complex than ever. What are the reasons? What are the effects? Problems and their repercussions are more multilayered, harder to understand. The different layers intermingle, making it impossible to get an overview of how things are related. Decisions are reduced to a tangled mesh of reaction and counterreaction, and choosing the single correct path is almost impossible.

Ambiguity: "One size fits all" and "best practice" have been relegated to yesterday. In today's world, it's rare for things to be completely clear or precisely determinable. Not everything is black and white—gray is also an option. The demands on modern organizations and management are more contradictory and paradoxical than ever, challenging our personal value systems to the core. In a world where the "what?" takes a back seat to the "why?" and the "how?" making decisions requires courage, awareness, and a willingness to make mistakes.

As I learned more about their VUCA curriculum, I became aware that although most of us are not functioning in the midst of a firefight, the principles of management and success remained the same. My intention with the stories in this book is to contemporize and extrapolate the learnings that took place for me over the course of thousands of hours of managing intense scenarios so as to be more prepared for the next one.

When I'm deep in the woods, mountains, or oceans, I am constantly and acutely aware of the dance that is taking place in front of me between order and chaos. The woods catch fire and renew. The mountains shed snow with avalanches and glaciers melt. The oceans rise and fall with the weather. At times, it seems tenuous at best, but deep down, I know that over millions of years, the natural court of checks and balances does a damn right-solid job at maintaining stability. That being said, our species is doing its best to sabotage those efforts on a grand scale in order to soften the edges of hard living. Through technological, scientific, and medical advancements, we are making life easier and doing our best to mitigate chaos and challenges. Food, shelter, and medical access are fairly accessible for the majority of us (the inequities of the socioeconomic class structure are a topic for an entirely different book), and all of us best be grateful for this and fully embrace it. By no means am I knocking or minimizing our efforts to improve quality of life; I'm just acutely aware that by doing so, we are now interpreting the world as a much more comfortable place than even our great grandparents did. Life expectancy in modern nations is double what it was a mere one hundred years ago. Our species continues to strive to take the disorder away from the playing field, all the while, the planet continues to adjust itself to our influence. By doing so, we are softening our calluses that are useful when the going gets tough. But my guess is, long after the human race has had its time on this rock, the Earth will quickly get back to reestablishing its own natural equilibrium. Without humans injecting our brand of security and "balance," the planet will find its genuine poise with chaos and order.

But for now, despite our grandest efforts to soften the blow of the challenging panorama of life, the only certainty for us is still relative uncertainty. It's relative in the sense that the "primitive" indigenous villager hunting wild boar in the jungles of Venezuela has a very different spectrum of VUCA issues than that of the Wall Street bond trader. Either one of these individuals would tell you that their set of daily assaults is just as valid as the other one. And therein lies the validity of it all. Each of us interprets change and chaos subjectively, and it carries the same personal weight.

In the present day, we typically encounter more innocuous challenges as opposed to the prior set of issues: wild animals, widespread famine, and natural disasters. But for those of us living in First World conditions (most everyone reading this book), I would dare to say that, in fact, our current society finds itself in a status of complacency. Contemporary life is relatively physically easy with only situational perceived chaos, and as a result, the conventional view of good and bad is fairly rigid. No longer are we threatened by large cats and bears if we choose not to be. Our hunting and foraging instincts are diluted to a point where the most challenging aspect of gathering food rests on whether to purchase two percent or whole milk. Humanity thrives on the pretense that order is the principle that guides us because we are constantly, deliberately navigating through a nearly manufactured life. The world is what it is. It most certainly is not as we wish it to be. Discomfort is the price of admission for a deeper, meaningful life. Tough situations are our binding contract for the life that we want to grow into. Every single day still provides us a new set of variables to interpret, juggle, and manage.

It's how we perceive the world around us that sets the table at which we dine. What optic do we use with regard to chaos, adversity, and uncertainty? Are we fearful? Hesitant? Reserved?

Each of us answers those questions uniquely, and, invariably, the answer can change from one day to the next. Our situational and emotional statuses greatly impact how we express our relationship to chaos and order.

How do you feel when you hear the word "order?" If you're like me and have somewhat of a rebellious streak in you, then you may feel repulsed. You may think of a Mussolini-styled autocrat, or perhaps a version of the *1984* "Big Brother" will come to mind. How about when you hear the word "chaos?" If you have a conservative side to your personality, you may feel repulsed. You may think of the breakdown of society—violence and looting in the streets.

But if you are rebellious and hear the word "chaos," you may think of the rejuvenating chaos of revolution—of change. Chaos that tears down the corrupt and tyrannical order. If you are conservative and hear the word "order" you may think of the benevolent and caring aspect of society and culture—the feeling of safety within the known territory, with the unknown dangers kept at bay.

Some people tend to swing toward one or the other extreme. And yes, the two are not separate categories—they are two extremes of one continuum. Think of the gradient illustration below with one end as the orderly or "less chaotic" end and the other as the chaotic or "less orderly" end.

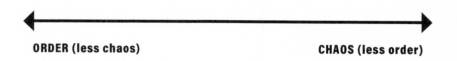

ORDER (less chaos)   **CHAOS (less order)**

A healthy society, and for that matter, a healthy individual is a balance between chaos and order. The chaos prevents stagnation, brings in novelty, and allows you to adapt to a wide variety of situations. The order gives you a foundation to operate out of and reflects the safety of known territory. But order can stagnate and become suffocating. It can lure you into zones of comfort and complacency. It can stifle growth and prevent you from adapting to change. Chaos can get out of hand and become destructive. Chaos can drag you down into the pits of despair. It can throw you into the unknown where you have no idea what to make of anything anymore.

So, what can we hope for as we trek through the ebb and flow of our journey? To be appreciative of the calm moments and be capable of accelerating to cover more ground when things are coming at you at a kinder, gentler pace. And then handling the tougher times with the resolution and fortitude necessary to forge forward in a graceful way, with a tough chin and a commitment to seeing it through. Either way, aiming toward forward progress.

I have found that in the midst of an "off the tracks" moment, I perform more effectively if I have something to shoot for—a plan, a direction, an intention. When you have something to concentrate on, your mind can remain focused, no matter what's happening. With a focused mind, when there is some kind of problem or you're clearly in a hazardous situation and you need to do something, you will know what the next step is. If you sit and stew on the conundrum and all the badness that exists within it, a paralyzing terror will envelop your headspace, leaving you incapable of formulating a plan. Some folks rush into problem-solving without taking time to think through all the possible solutions, and they screw it up. Resist being impulsive. Consult with your team. Sometimes you have to "go slow to go fast." When you have the next step in mind, then you have something to focus on. Maybe what's next is just a baby step. That'll do. Maybe you are so out of your depth that the next step is to ask for help. That's actually a good one. You don't need to fix everything in one fell swoop. You just need to know your next step, and you can keep it together. Now when you consider your next step, you want to think technically and specifically to resist panic.

When you think about it in those terms, which are to get away from the label of what this situation is and then get into what is technically going on here, then it's a lot easier to adjust. Then you don't get focused on the fear. You get focused on, "What's my next step?" The cards have been dealt. Now it's time for me to play those cards to the best of my ability. Rob Harsh is the personification of this mentality.

Rob had been an adventuring partner of mine for close to twenty years when he called us all together at a restaurant in Boulder one evening to inform this close group of friends that he had recently been diagnosed with Stage 4 lung cancer. This was one of those mind-bending stories about a freakishly athletic young man who had never held a cigarette to his mouth and not even had an inkling of cancer in his family lineage. It was a jaw-dropping announcement full of sadness and disbelief. Rob seemed to be the only one in the room who wasn't crying. He assured us, as most newly diagnosed cancer patients do, that he would fight this thing with all he had and we were not to fret. Having been witness to Rob handling adversity in the field like an absolute warrior, it occurred to me that if anybody could do it, Rob would be the guy. Boy, was I right.

He decided on the day of his diagnosis that he would not play the role of the victim. No time to feel sorry for himself. He would immediately commence researching alternative, naturopathic treatment strategies for his particular strain of cancer. It became his full-time job as he immersed himself deep into the subject matter and oftentimes found himself more up to speed on current therapies than several of the oncologists he was consulting. He listened to his body, stayed calm, and leaned in on his support network of friends and family. His cocktail of therapies and approach toward the illness provided him with seismic news just two years after his initial diagnosis: his full-body scan showed no active tumors. He was one-hundred percent clean.

Rob's approach to the most life-bending news was both courageous and methodical. We are all convinced that it was his elastic and resilient mindset that propelled him through such a tumultuous landscape. He fully committed himself to his healing with no time for passivity. He would be the active conductor in determining a strategy, executing the treatment plan, and emotionally standing his ground against this physical intruder. The cancer didn't have a chance.

The external variables of life surely dictate how we attempt to establish equilibrium. But there is also a deep-seated evolutionary response to the barrage of worldly input: our hormones. To understand how they impact us, it's important to appreciate the role of each hormone, why it's generated, and what its action is on our emotional well-being. If we have a deeper understanding of their roles, we are better suited to positively impact our teammates and communities as we navigate the complexities of life.

When I consider these hormones, the big players consist of endorphins, dopamine, serotonin, oxytocin, and cortisol. This grouping of impactful hormones has a massive influence on how we relate to the world and all of its assaults, both positive and negative. Several of them somewhat overlap, but on a fundamental level, there are some slight nuances.

First and foremost: endorphins, probably the most well known of the hormones. Endorphins are fundamentally designed to do one thing, and that's mask pain. I think it goes without saying that endorphins are one of the main influencers on why every species is able to continue procreating with regards to females and the birthing process. During labor and delivery, women are flooded with endorphins; otherwise the pain would be overwhelming, and a woman would be like, "Hell no, I'm not having sex." Because what happens when you have sex? You get pregnant. What happens when you get pregnant? You have a baby, and it hurts like hell. Endorphins have allowed us and countless other species to perpetuate life.

Endorphins also mask pain for endurance. To be able to track animals for hours, early humans had to have these endorphins to stay in the fight for extended hunts. We needed to have the ability to mask the pain when we hurt, to continue on despite physical pain. When it all comes crashing down, and we've amputated our leg, and we're a guy named Matt Nyman, the Delta Force guy who was on our first Warriors expedition (see Chapter 5), we're flooded with endorphins. Nyman's leg got cut off by a propeller blade and was lying on the other side of a rooftop. He still had the ability to reach over and grab his morphine, stab himself in the leg, and then pull his weapon up and start shooting to be able to protect the guys who are on that rooftop with him. Endorphins are obviously a major player in the tapestry of our chemical evolution and well-being and play a major role in how we handle adversity.

Then, there's dopamine. Dopamine makes you feel good. We get a flood of dopamine when we achieve something, when we hit the target. We get it when we have a list and knock items off, one by one. I make these lists all the time in my mind, and whenever I accomplish something on that list and I cross it off, I get a little shot of dopamine. Or you put a post on Facebook, and you get numerous likes. With each positive affirmation, you get a little shot of dopamine. From an evolutionary perspective, dopamine has been crucial for hunting and gathering. Our early ancestors would see a fruit tree or an antelope off in the distance and get an immediate shot of dopamine. It's not hunger that drove them to the tree or the animal; it's the chemical reward that runs parallel to the knowledge that if I work hard to close the distance to that food, I will be fed. The dopamine provides us small chemical prizes as we pursue large scale, sustainable goals, even if they are fraught with complexities.

There is also a dark side to dopamine that accompanies its secretion, and that is its highly addictive nature. We get shots of dopamine from drugs, gambling, and alcohol, and from Facebook likes, checking our cell phones, buying and selling stocks, and doing all the countless tasks that fill our days. At some point, we learn to manufacture dopamine hits. We seek them in an artificial way because they feel good to us. This can, over time, become self-destructive. I believe that if we are armed with the knowledge around the infusion of dopamine, we can be more mindful in looking for dopamine hits in constructive and organic ways as opposed to seeking them out in artificial or inefficient pathways.

Both endorphins and dopamine are generated in our bodies, primarily on a subjective and individual scale. This means my actions alone can dictate the levels at which these hormones are introduced. However, there are some other big hormone players that rely more on external input to flood themselves into our consciousness. Serotonin and oxytocin become the power brokers as we engage with others. They are the playground hormones.

I think of serotonin as more or less like the teamwork chemical. It contributes to our sense of pride and our status within the group. It contributes to those feelings that surround your kids, spouse, teammates, and the people you're sharing an experience with. We need serotonin to be able to reinforce relationships, and, undoubtedly, nurturing relationships should be considered the most worthy exercise we undertake as a species. We get shots of serotonin from being a part of something that's positive, powerful, and bigger than us as individuals. It encourages us to align with other individuals and partnerships, and as we do so, we find comfort, power, and a thorough bathing in serotonin.

Studies have shown that within all primate groups (and countless other species for that matter), failing to identify with a group, family, or team dynamic results in a steep drop in serotonin and, as a result, a degradation of that individual's general well-being. "Groupless" individuals not associated with a multimember tribe become emotionally labile and fairly ineffective at common daily tasks. We all crave the unity and cohesiveness that accompanies being a part of a team, and much of this is a result of our underlying quest for serotonin infusions. This has become a critical piece of science within the veteran community and is translatable to the civilian space as well.

While serving, our soldiers, marines, and airmen feel that they are a part of something much bigger than themselves as individuals. They are constantly flooded with serotonin while on active duty. Once they return to civilian life, the bigger meaning is lost, and so is the constant source of serotonin. Their serotonin drops from these highly elevated levels to negligible levels, and then they find themselves sitting in their mom's basement playing PlayStation, drinking whiskey, and taking pills. They've lost a sense of belonging, so they abruptly decompensate.

Sebastien Junger writes extensively about this topic in his book *Tribe* (a highly recommended read). Comprehending and applying this concept is critical in the treatment of veteran PTSD and depression. We have seen this time and time again in our Warriors program and, as a result, we focus on reengaging veterans and aiding them to reidentify purpose and community. The most significant missing element in civilian life is that connection to their tribe. When the tribe is lost, so is the abundance of serotonin.

Next on the heavy hitter hormone list is oxytocin. I like to think of it as the "giver hormone." We get blasts of oxytocin when we lend of ourselves to someone else. We do something nice for someone…nice little shot of the "tocin." We give someone a gift for a birthday or Christmas; they get the gift, and we get the tocin. It is literally derived from being of service to others, so we could think of it as the servant leader chemical. The servant leaders of the world have tapped into this powerful feedback loop, and the world is a better place because of that. Oxytocin can be a treasure chest if sought after as a leader and can be a constant source of positive feedback for burgeoning leaders in tough times.

Finally, there's the one that I think really impacts us the most as it relates to this VUCA world—cortisol. Cortisol is the stress and anxiety hormone. It injects itself into our bodies whenever we are stressed, scared, anxious, and/or fearful. Evolutionarily, it has been paramount in its ability to equip us in the fight or flight scenarios. Saber-tooth tiger on the horizon…acute blast of cortisol…run like hell. When we don't feel safe, cortisol prompts glucose to be injected into our muscles, and we are promptly ready to fire off at a moment's notice. Cortisol can keep us alive. I have certainly had my share of cortisol blasts while perched on the flanks of a big scary mountain, and for sure owe a debt of gratitude to cortisol for providing me the juice to escape from many of those tenuous situations.

That being said, cortisol is a component that is most effective in short bursts, not long burns like many of us are subjected to in our current social framework. We now operate in these stressful contexts where we receive long, sustained injections of cortisol secondary to being exposed to stresses at work or at home. Our never-ending news cycle tells us to be concerned and worried about everything. Our calendars are chock full of meetings and obligations that require a certain baseline of stress to accomplish. Over time, this abundance of cortisol leads to high blood pressure, diabetes, cardiovascular disease, hair loss, and guys—it even causes your balls to shrink.

This steady-state, low-dose cortisol potion that ebbs through our bodies during periods of stress, hovering for these long-extended periods, can also keep us from managing adversity effectively. Many of us allow the anxiety and fear associated with cortisol injections to run amok with our critical decision-making. We become irrational and blow a gasket when, in fact, these are the moments we need to remain the most calm.

Cortisol management skills are worthy of pursuing for all of us. I am a big advocate in the practices of yoga, meditation, and breathing exercises, and using these mind calisthenics to help our bodies return back to the steady state of calm effectiveness. Adjusting our baseline of calm in everyday life gives us the ability to do a hard reset when things feel like they are becoming unhinged.

The cocktail of these hormones has a heavy internal influence on how we operate in our own personal snow globes. The regular infusion of hormones guides our decisions, moods, and physical well-being. Understanding and comprehending the function of each of these hormones and relating to them as you are feeling and experiencing can provide solid insight into how you might amplify your actions and/ or adjust your attitude to maintain that desired equilibrium. "I'm stressed" equals too much cortisol. Pause, adjust, refocus, adapt, and purge the cortisol to allow more serotonin in. Being cognizant of the balance gives you more clarity on how you can absolutely tweak your mental state.

Another potential hack for interpreting chaos is to simply change the entire nature and narrative of how we perceive the constant barrage of VUCA events. The method here is giving each one of the terms to a more positive spin. I have found that some of us perform better when we change the subjective perspective, tilting towards the optimistic plane.

In that spirit…the flipped VUCA model:

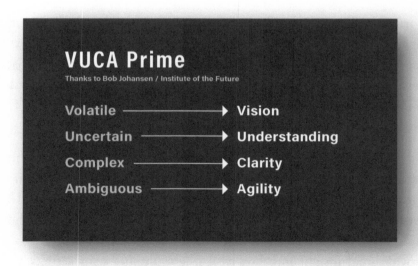

VUCA Prime
Thanks to Bob Johansen / Institute of the Future

Volatile ⟶ Vision

Uncertain ⟶ Understanding

Complex ⟶ Clarity

Ambiguous ⟶ Agility

Counter Volatility with Vision. Once it becomes clear that you are headed into a volatile scenario that is fraught with instability, a quick pivot over to the planning and vision approach gives all who are involved a sense of purpose. We are actively acknowledging the volatility and are committed to the planning phase for how we will manage the issue.

Meet Uncertainty with Understanding. By establishing an "in the know" environment, you improve your ability to anticipate threats and take advantage of new opportunities. You are keenly aware of the uncertain landscape that lies before you, and you are ready and prepared to interpret it for what it is.

React to Complexity with Clarity. A convoluted and complex setting should be met with a crystal-clear message. You are meeting confusion with lucidity and, by doing so, stealing the stage from the confusion, not adding fuel to it. The other members of your team will find solace and inspiration in a clear direction and are encouraged to move onto the solution stage of the issue.

Fight Ambiguity with Agility. Embracing emotional flexibility and adaptability during uncertain times teaches us to go with the flow and shuns the rigid nature that can impede creative outcomes. Remaining open to options and being able to quickly pivot gives us the platform to address vague and undefined issues.

Sometimes all it takes is an intentional shift in perception to embolden us. The flipped VUCA model is another tool to be placed in the management quiver. It's another method for strengthening emotional agility and constructing a method of adapting the mindset necessary for both the peaks and the valleys.

The magic sauce will have a different flavor for every one of us. Whether you are better served redefining what VUCA looks like in a more positive light, or perhaps you work more effectively by establishing a focal point to be that North Star as a guiding point, we need to develop the tools that work best for us subjectively. What has become clear to me over the years is that sitting back and hoping that things get clarified or wishing that they just get better is simply a form of apathy that delays the process of recalibration.

My hope is that through the sharing of these stories, you will find your own method of handling VUCA events in your life and can lean in to those moments, knowing full well that with a healthy and aware mindset, the tornadoes that swoop out of the sky are manageable, and you will undoubtedly find a way to transcend the storm.

A younger Jeff balancing his inner chaos

Chapter 2: Lessons from Mosul

"Chaos is the law of nature; Order is the dream of man."
— **Henry Adams**

As soon as the third mortar struck fifty feet outside our trauma bay, we knew ISIS was directly targeting us. The shrapnel shot out at high velocity, a large chunk striking one of our paramedics in the back of the leg and sending him to the ground. We all hustled into our makeshift bunker, which was, in more peaceful times, a living room in a private home complete with couches and a table. We listened as the debris rained down on to the corrugated roof outside the bunker. The smell of acrid smoke wafted into our space. It had been a constant orchestra of small arms fire and explosions all around us for weeks. The entire scene was now eerily quiet.

The first incoming mortar had landed twenty minutes earlier, about one hundred feet from our position. We knew from the sound of the explosion and the rattling of the walls around us that this one was different from the hundreds of rounds that had been outgoing around us for weeks now. This one was coming in, and it was close. That being said, we knew we were close to the front line in the middle of a combat zone, and random mortars can land anywhere at any time. We paused for a second and then got back to work taking care of the four or five patients who were prone on our trauma beds, each of them with significant penetrating trauma.

Then ten minutes later, the second one struck, seventy-five feet from our position.

Damn.

That was close enough to feel the shock of the blast. It sent a ripple of fear through all nine of us. Two incoming mortars within ten minutes seemed strange.

But it wasn't until number three hit that shit got real. It was at that moment that we realized this was an intentional grid. The mortars were progressively coming closer, and the next one could be the last one they needed to accomplish their goal. We all moved toward the back wall of the "bunker," and a few nervous laughs fluttered up.

Then someone caught sight of several members of our security detail carrying in the lifeless body of one of our special operations security guards. They dumped one of the Iraqi Special Operations Forces (ISOF) soldiers, Asbad, on one of our trauma beds and screamed for help.

Three months prior to Asbad's body being dropped onto my trauma bed in Mosul, I received a call from Phil Suarez, one of the founders of a world-class Non-Governmental Organization (NGO) called NYC Medics (www.nycmedics.org). I had met Phil two years prior as I was preparing to deploy with NYC Medics immediately following the devastating earthquake that took place in Nepal that killed close to 10,000 people (more on that later). Phil told me that he had an "interesting" assignment bestowed on them by the World Health Organization and wanted to know if I would use my twenty years of experience as an emergency medicine physician assistant to lead a team of nurses and paramedics. He mentioned something about Iraq…ISIS…front lines…combat zone…high volume of penetrating trauma.

Sweet. I'm in.

Turns out, I probably should have asked my wife.

The initial pushback from Merry Beth was pretty heavy. My first pitch to her that I wanted to go to Iraq to volunteer in a combat zone didn't go over too well. She knew what she was getting into fourteen years prior when she agreed to marry an international mountain guide, and she was quite prepared for the biannual, two-month-long climbing expeditions that I typically jaunted off on to the Himalaya or Andes. But this was totally different and "not cool."

I explained to her that this would be a unique experience for me to work in a theater that was new to me and would challenge me in new and interesting ways. I would be able to practice high-level trauma medicine for the first time in a while, and I would be embracing an opportunity to lead a team in a chaotic environment, something I gravitate toward.

"That's all great and exciting, honey…but how about the fact that the most evil dudes in the world would only be a few hundred yards from you and would love nothing more than to kill a handful of Americans that are aiding their enemy. How about that?"

She had a good point.

I passed along to her the same safety criteria that Phil had provided me. I assured her that we would have high-level security surrounding us at all times, and that we would actually be directly embedded with the Iraqi ISOF. And in fact, it was our own U.S. Special Operations teams that trained ISOF. So these guys are the best of the best. High-level operators. No problem. Safe as can be.

The old, "respect my spouse's wishes but still be true to myself" balancing act. I'm fairly familiar with this particular syndrome, but sometimes it is more profound than others.

Over the next week, we discussed the proposition. We brought our eleven-year-old son into the conversation and listened to his concerns. I canvassed several of my Ranger, Delta, and SEAL buddies who had all spent time in the "sandbox." Generally, I heard, "Dude, why on Earth would you want to go over there? It's a shitty, dangerous place. Just stay home safe with your family."

I Googled my way down the "ISIS in Mosul" rabbit hole to gain some clarity on who was fighting whom and why. I learned that ISIS had swooped into Mosul in 2014 and almost overnight claimed "possession" of both East and West Mosul. At the time, there was very little pushback as the Iraqi Army and Federal Police (Fed Pol) were caught with their pants down and provided no push back. Several years later, supported by our own US military, the ISOF, and Fed Pol were taking the fight to ISIS in an effort to retake the city of Mosul. The east side of the Tigris River was secured, and the Kurds had reestablished it as "Kurdish" territory. Now the Iraqis were fighting to win back their half of the city. We would be embedded with ISOF and provide direct trauma support for ISOF/Fed Pol and the occasional civilian caught in the crossfire.

My SEAL Team 6 buddy hit me with something that had lasting power. He said, "Okay, I know you. I know you've already made up your mind that you're going, and there's nothing anyone can say or do to keep you from going. So, let's get you as prepared and capable as you can be so that you come back in one piece."

That was a man who knew how to operate within the scope of realities, and that's why he served in the highest level of warfare and intelligence for close to two decades. I will always be grateful to him for his insight and the contributions he provided to our teams as we prepared to deploy.

It wasn't that I didn't heed everyone else's advice and input. I valued the opinions of everyone I talked with about it. I chocked away every suggestion and commentary that I was provided, knowing that each tidbit could be useful at some juncture. But the crux of whether to go or not was going to be based on my own personal dive into my motives. As I've grown and matured, I've learned to do an honest self-inventory on what my intentions are with every action I take. This clearly hasn't always been the case, especially in my more spontaneous and void-of-consequences approach to my twenties and thirties. I suppose most of us have made this metamorphosis as the years pass, some of us more expeditiously than others. I'm on the "mid-forties figure it out plan."

In this case, I had to truthfully ask myself: why am I really doing this? Is it to get my thrill-seeking rocks off in some way? Is it to fill some guilty void for not serving in the military when I easily could have? Is it to have more subject matter to write about in a book?

In that self-discovery phase (some call it prayer, some call it thought meditation, some call it self-reflection. I call it lifting the hood), I will typically find the answer. Sometimes I'll like it. Occasionally not. And either way is okay. What's important is to ask those questions.

For this particular mission, I suppose it was a little of all of those posits. However, I truly felt committed in my mind that taking on this mission was the right thing to do. Although I felt no particular affinity for the Iraqi people in the way that I do the Nepali, I still felt obligated to do my part to make the world a better place. And that by helping a group of warriors take the fight to pure evil, I could at least contribute in a small way.

Oh…and I kinda wanted to get my thrill-seeking rocks off a bit too.

Upon landing in Erbil, Iraq, in the spring of 2017, I was introduced to my team, a collection of highly seasoned New York City paramedics and critical care nurses. Although the personalities varied from gregariously outspoken to quiet and mousey, we all seemed to generally get along, especially once the work began in earnest.

That first evening, as we made the drive from the airport in Irbil across the Tigris River over to West Mosul, we entered the combat zone. Multiple Humvees were being dragged and towed back from the front lines, all of them inoperable, blown to pieces. Ambulances screamed away from the front lines carrying the dead and injured. Apache helicopters buzzed overhead firing out dozens of 70 mm rocket rounds just a couple of miles away. A fleet of trucks with mounted rocket launchers was parked a half mile away, constantly sending off "lob rockets," basically 107 mm ass-thumping missiles. We all found ourselves ducking whenever an outgoing round would shake the ground as it fired off.

As we were getting the handoff from the outgoing medical team we were replacing, the new patients started pouring in. A five-year-old girl got placed on an open trauma bed screaming in agony. I quickly determined that she had a through and through gunshot to the hip. Fortunately, it appeared the bullet had missed her vital organs, but the pain was absolutely immense. Beside her lay an Iraqi Federal Police officer (a sort of second-tier Iraqi soldier) who had also been shot, blood pouring from his leg. Large outgoing rounds continued to shake the building with small arms fire zinging off within a few hundred yards. This was all within twenty minutes of arriving at our trauma stabilization point (TSP).

Welcome to Mosul.

The days flew by with dozens of casualties each day, mostly military and a handful of civilians. The fighting would start right after the morning call to prayer. My morning routine: choke down some oatmeal, sip on some Nescafé, and watch the fireworks show kickoff. Typically, within thirty minutes of the first few explosions, we would receive our first ambulance. Gunshot wound to the abdomen. Then another: IED explosion, lower extremity amputation. And another: multiple gunshot wounds to the thorax. And so on and so on.

Our team worked heroically and tirelessly day after day. Just as a patient was packaged and moved on to the next level of care or placed in a body bag, the blood mopped from underneath the bed, and the equipment restocked, another ambulance would scream in with several more critical patients. All the while, the report of continuous explosions could be heard from nearby positions.

After a little over a week of a fairly constant flow of high acuity trauma, the volume started to wane. Although we appreciated a mild respite, we knew we were there for a job and wanted to be in a position to aid as many casualties as possible. And right on cue, the head of ISOF, General Athar Abbas stopped by our trauma base and sat down for a powwow with Kathy, our head of logistics and operations. After what appeared to be a rather lengthy and detailed discussion, Kathy gathered up our team and presented us with an option.

The front line was advancing. Although the toll was high, ISOF was pushing ISIS back, city block by city block. If we wanted to be within that ten-minute golden window of saving lives impacted by severe trauma, we would need to move forward to follow the fight.

"How close to the front line?" I asked.

"Five hundred meters," Kathy replied.

A collective "Whoa!" went up from the group.

Kathy went on to explain that ISOF had identified and secured a trauma base for us in the garage area of an abandoned home, and we would be setting up residence in a different home across the street from the trauma bay. Both the residence and the trauma bay would have access to concrete reinforced subterranean bunkers. And now, there would be an even higher level of security detail surrounding us 24/7.

The deliberation amongst the team was brief. We knew what we had to do. Twenty-four hours later, we were rolling out in a twenty-five-vehicle convoy of trucks, Humvees, and Jeeps with all of our medical gear, trauma beds, and personal effects loaded up.

Immediately after pulling up on the street outside of our new digs, it became clear to us all—this was different. We were now really in the shit. Instead of hearing exclusively outgoing rounds, we could now discern the difference between incoming and outgoing rounds. Turns out, impacting ordinance makes a much different sound than a round firing off. The rockets that the Apaches were letting loose were landing MUCH closer now. The smells, the smoke, and the sound were all turned up to eleven. The fighting was four or five solid tee shots away.

A day later, our makeshift trauma bay was all set up, and patients began flooding in. Ambulances and Humvees would screech up in front of our trauma bay, and several soldiers would then carry in semiconscious and sometimes lifeless bodies and plop them on our beds. We would secure the airway, stop the bleeding, and intervene where we had to. In many cases, it was enough; in many others, it was not.

Day three rolled around, and things started to get weird. Around noon, thousands of civilians started walking down the street away from the combat zone. They had all been logjammed for days several hundred meters away as the Federal Police and ISOF did "background checks" on everyone and even fingerprinted fighting-age males to determine whether they were on a supposed ISIS sympathizer list. Once the gate was opened, an endless stream of displaced locals ambled down the dirt road one hundred meters from our position. We watched with a mix of sadness, pity, and an urge to help. But, I'm not gonna lie—we also felt fear. Our "Spidey" senses went to full tingle mode with the thought that any of these civilians could run toward us at any moment and wreak havoc with a suicide vest. Not gonna lie, being so close to the front lines in the middle of a combat zone and watching a man carry a huge piece of "luggage" down the dirt road, right toward you, is a bit unsettling. We did our best to trust the system and focus on the work in front of us.

From time to time, a family of civilians would be permitted to walk toward us carrying and, in some cases, pushing a loved one who had been shot or injured from shrapnel. Oftentimes, these injuries were over twenty-four hours old, and in some cases already gangrenous.

We continued to be vigilant, expressing our concerns to the head of our security team. Haseeb dutifully listened and nodded approvingly, but this was a man who had grown up in a war-ravaged Iraq and seemed fairly calloused to the proximity of combat and threat. He reassured us that we would be fine; no person would be permitted through the checkpoint unless they had been thoroughly screened, and absolutely no civilians would be allowed into our space unless their injuries were life-threatening and they had been cleared of weapons.

It was evident that we were experiencing a variation in subjective optics. Haseeb was not sensing that the situation was at all ominous, whereas the Americans all felt like the scene was spiraling out of control, destined for chaos. This discrepancy in perspective is a common occurrence in life and can frequently lead to conflict. Truly listening and being effectively heard both require a deft set of diplomacy skills built by years of dealing with complex relationships. In this case, Haseeb was the expert, and it was his experience and voice that we would lean on. We just needed him to listen to us and the reservations that we were feeling.

When I reflect back on this, this moment was undoubtedly a critical juncture for us as a team. We had been presented information, details, and data, and were asked to interpret it and make a decision that would change our trajectory greatly. Although this is a fairly extreme version of this scenario, the value of this moment and what went into it is pertinent for countless, less life-threatening deliberations. Listening to teammates, establishing a healthy dialogue, and collaboratively deciding the next steps are critical in group decision-making with dense objectives. We intuitively took these steps and made our call. We rallied around Haseeb and the team, lifted our chins up, and committed to the mission. For better or worse.

Day four in our forward position dawned for me after five hours of fitful sleep. I stepped outside the residence with my cup of coffee to take in the scene and greet the security guard, Asbad, who was posted up by our front gate. We were exchanging broken Arabic/English morning salutations when a civilian male came running through the security perimeter with a lifeless little girl in his arms. The team quickly mobilized and ran across the street to the trauma bay, where the little girl had been laid. The father was inconsolable. His daughter had been shot in the back of the head by an ISIS sniper twenty minutes prior as they were fleeing for the safety of ISOF-controlled terrain. There was nothing we could do. I will never forget the sound of the father's wailing in what can only be described as the worst scenario any parent can ever imagine.

I stepped away from the bed, and for the first time since arriving in Iraq, I cried. It felt as though I had placed a restrictor cap on my emotions in order to operate effectively in such a chaotic and violent atmosphere. And now I had to let it out. We all did, but not for long. I wiped away the tears as the first Humvee screamed around the corner and dropped two patients at our door. It was 7:30 a.m. on a Tuesday.

Early afternoon hit, and the fighting seemed to intensify. Dozens of patients came in and out, with a high level of immense, penetrating trauma.

Then the first mortar struck. We flinched.

Mortar number two slammed down ten minutes later. We cringed.

Mortar number three exploded fifty feet away, and we knew that we had just crested into the realm of directly being targeted. They knew we were there, and they were coming for us. As the debris was still raining down on the tin garage roof, we all took refuge in the bunker with a clear view out into the trauma bay and the entrance to the street.

Smoke still hung in the air as I noticed a group of soldiers carrying what appeared to be the lifeless body of another soldier. They were screaming, "Musaeada! Musaeada!" Arabic for "Help!"

Even from ten meters away, I could recognize the face of the limp body they were carrying. It was our security guard and friend, Asbad, and he appeared to be dead.

It was one of those moments when everything slows down and becomes very still. Although chaos is raining down from every angle, the optic with which you are viewing the scene becomes quiet and clear. I'm familiar with these moments. I've experienced them in the big mountains of Alaska and the Himalaya. Essentially, life gets distilled down into a basic question: go or don't go? We stay in the relatively safe confines of the bunker and wait out the barrage, or we charge out into the maelstrom and execute the job we have been tasked to do.

Perhaps some of us are wired in charge mode. I'm uncertain if that is a good thing or not, but what I do know is that, for better or worse, I have been blasting into situations for most of my life, and more often than not, it has served me well. But the instant question that hung in the space around me was whether I would ask my team to step out of the relative safety of the bunker and attempt to work on Asbad. One of the axioms that Brigadier General Thomas A. Kolditz provides in his book, *In Extremis Leadership,* is that a leader should never share any less risk than their teammates. Essentially, never ask anyone to do anything you aren't willing to do first. I secured my Kevlar vest and helmet and stepped up from the bunker.

The smoke and dust hadn't even settled from the mortar strike. The sounds of screaming and small arms fire were bouncing around under our corrugated roof, adding to an extremely hectic scene. Without a spoken word, the team moved in unison, right behind me, through the door of the bunker out into the chaos. We surrounded Asbad and quickly began assessing his condition. He had a faint pulse, pale skin, muted respirations, and was completely unresponsive. He was, for all intents and purposes, dead.

After he was stripped down, I identified an entry wound in his upper right chest. It wasn't particularly large, but with the limited breath sounds from that right lung, I was suspicious that he had what's called a hemothorax. This condition is a buildup of blood in the pleural space (lung cavity) that ultimately inhibits the lung from fully inflating with respirations. In this case, a piece of shrapnel from the mortar had pierced Asbad's chest wall and caused massive amounts of bleeding into the space where his lung would typically expand.

The prognosis for a profound hemothorax? You die.

In an acute trauma scenario, the treatment for this condition is to cut a hole into the chest cavity, place a tube inside the pleural space and drain the blood out so the lung can get back to normal function. I quickly cleaned the space between Asbad's fourth and fifth rib, and grabbed a scalpel. I made the incision, inserted my finger into Asbad's chest cavity, and immediately got doused with at least a liter of blood as it evacuated all over me and onto the dirty concrete floor. Like the scene from *Pulp Fiction* when Uma Thurman's character springs back to life, Asbad dramatically took the first full breath he'd had in several minutes as the blood dripped from my elbow.

A couple of hours after resuscitating Asbad, we emerged from our bunker and were quickly evacuated in a couple of bullet-sprayed Humvees back to our old clinic site well out of reach from the ISIS mortars. That evening as we gathered around a small campfire in the front yard of our clinic/home and the adrenaline finally ebbed out of our bodies, we were informed that an ISIS operative had slipped through the security checkpoint and positioned himself in an abandoned home just three houses down from our clinic site. Turns out, he was intermittently releasing pigeons to show our position to his asshole colleagues 500 meters away. He would release a bird, and five minutes later, a mortar would be released. He would then text adjustments to the bad guys and then release another pigeon. And so on and so on. Once we were safely evacuated, our ISOF guys captured him and were able to conduct a full interrogation. He admitted his efforts and, with great vitriol, claimed he wanted to help kill the infidel doctors who were aiding his enemy. We were told he was dealt with "the Iraqi way." We didn't ask for any more details.

Several days after I got home, I was yearning for quiet and stillness, so I went out on a trail run deep in the hills with my wife. I had been feeling scattered and solemn since returning home and found myself ruminating on the same emotions I had heard so many times from my veteran friends. Depression, fear, and anxiety all mishmashed in with gratitude and relief. I felt ashamed that I was experiencing these emotions after spending less than thirty days in a combat zone while many of my special operator pals have spent months and even years on multiple deployments in the middle of one shitshow after the next. In conversations with them, I was reassured that my experience was condensed, and the events I was a part of were concentrated and impactful. Like a glass of wine, they needed to breathe.

I charged up the long and windy hill with Merry Beth right behind. I felt powerful in spite of being in relatively crappy shape. All of the images and emotions pressed me up that hill. As I crested the top, I felt them welling up, and by the time I turned to my wife, I was sobbing. I laid my head on her shoulder and wept for who knows how long. No words were spoken. Just emotion escaping and flowing over the brim.

I'll be the first to admit that I am a man who is not afraid to show emotion, and when the time calls for it, let the tears flow. Intuitively, I guess, I have realized that plugging up intense emotions can be crippling. Our emotional equilibrium is based on the input and handling of feelings and emotions. Like an overinflated balloon, the pressure can build up to an unmanageable and dangerous state, and that's when the darkness can present itself in destructive ways. Bleeding out the pressure is a critical method for maintaining that healthy emotional balance. Research confirms that when we suppress our emotions or ignore them altogether, they get stronger. Psychologists refer to this as emotional amplification. The therapy for this is letting it out. Cry, scream, hit a punching bag, talk to a therapist. Just allow it to come out of you as opposed to keeping it cordoned off in an emotional cage. Whether it's having a good cry or a healthy sit-down dialogue with those who you are emotionally engaged with, allowing emotions to roam about the cabin in a healthy and constructive way is really good medicine for all involved.

How we operate in these volatile situations and environments is a direct cross section into who we are as individuals and teammates. It's not about being super tough in the face of adversity or hiding your fears from those around you. Real situations call for real emotion. Hiding or faking emotion can ultimately backfire and leave us gasping for air at critical junctures. It comes down to manifesting forward movement while still in the realm of uncertainty. Allowing the focus to be on what can be done as opposed to what can't be. Nurturing the good in the situation instead of allowing the dark to soak up the momentum. If executed effectively, growth is guaranteed.

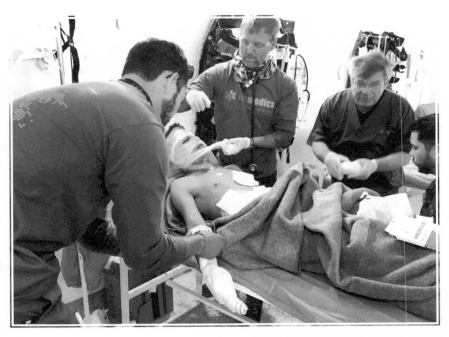

Jeff and the team doing the work in Mosul, Iraq.

Chapter 3: Everest with a Blind Guy . . . What Could Go Wrong?

"The best teamwork comes from men who are working independently toward one goal in unison."

— James Cash Penney

I stood at the edge of the crevasse and gazed down into what I imagined was the true definition of "bottomless." The ice wall below my boots fell away into an expansive black hole that slowly vapored into blackness. It looked as though if I happened to fall into this hole, I would have plenty of time to consider how deep it was prior to finally hitting bottom. In fact, the Sherpas say if you fall down into one of these deeper crevasses, you end up back in America.

It occurred to me at that moment that we always hear that hell is really a hot inferno. In this case, not so much. The cold, dark breeze that emanated up from this massive hole in the glacier sent shivers down my spine, knowing that with one wrong step, I would end up entombed deep inside the ice. And with one ill-stated command, my blind buddy would meet the same fate.

The entire crevasse stretched roughly sixty feet from my current position over to the other side. Six aluminum ladders latched to one another with some ratty looking polypropylene cord bridged the gap. Honestly, I probably wouldn't even trust tying my dog up to a fence post with this "rope." But it's what the Sherpas use, and, therefore, it's what we use. The rope is there less to catch you as it is to give you something to hold on to as you tiptoe across ladder after ladder after ladder. This particular stretch of ladders also had a nice little down and left tilt to it, just to add another level of spice.

Prior to the kickoff of any Himalayan climbing expedition, the team gathers for a blessing ceremony called a puja, which is typically administered by a revered and sage Buddhist monk. It takes place at base camp and is full of protective prayers, juniper smoke, singing bowls, chanting, and perhaps a little nip of local whiskey, all with the intention of requesting a safe and productive climb from Buddha, God, Mohammad, or whichever deity you are inclined to have a relationship with. In spite of the solemn nature of the proceedings, it is a happy and joyous occasion, full of laughter and excited spirits, oftentimes followed by a memorable hangover.

The monk who conducted our puja had provided each one of us climbers with a little handful of dried rice that he had blessed. It was magic rice, he told us. If we were ever in a situation on the mountain that felt particularly daunting, we should take a little sprinkle and throw it to the heavens for "extra" protection. I had stored mine away in an empty film canister and duct-taped it to the strap on my backpack for easy access.

I took one look at this behemoth of a crevasse...and proceeded to dump the entire canister straight down inside.

As I prepared to step on to the first rung of the ladder and commit to the crossing, I was keenly aware that Erik was "looking" at me to gauge my level of fear and concern. As I had seen him do in countless other precarious situations, he was intently listening to see if my breathing rate increased, if I became fidgety, or, perhaps, if I mumbled anything resembling a "shit, man." One of his remaining "senses" was that of situational assessment, which meant listening to his guide to gauge the level of scariness he was about to encounter.

I took a big deep breath, maybe even said a little prayer, and then stepped out over the abyss.

The Khumbu Icefall is the first order of business when climbing Everest. Just a twenty-minute walk up from base camp, it roars at you throughout the night while you attempt to sleep in your tent, asking you in your dreams if you've got the courage to venture up into its waiting grasp. The sound of crashing avalanches is the background music as you contemplate travel up into the yaw of the icefall. Undoubtedly, it's the deadliest section of the entire mountain, having claimed forty-six lives at last count. In 2014, a major serac, or ice tower, released from the upper flanks of the west shoulder of Everest, dropped down into the icefall, killing sixteen Sherpas in one fell swoop.

As the glacier drops from Camp I down to Everest Base Camp over a distance of about a half-mile, it gets squeezed between the west shoulder of Everest and the east face of a neighboring mountain called Nuptse. Huge seracs are formed , some teetering 200 feet in the air, precariously balancing and waiting for a shift in the glacier to send them exploding down. As the ice shifts, explodes, and calves off at an average of three feet per day, it engulfs whatever or whoever is currently climbing in its labyrinth. It's not unusual for a section of ladders and fixed ropes to get buried the very next day after being installed. It is the epitome of chaos, a jumbled-up deathtrap of a maze.

Guiding Erik through this deadly gauntlet was proving to be the hardest thing I had ever done in my life. Every step, every move was consequential for the both of us. By the time we encountered this massive crevasse that I currently stood over, we had crossed at least a dozen smaller versions that had, in a way, prepared us for this particular ice canyon. Moments before, Erik grumbled up at me, "Dude, this place does not suit the Americans with Disability Act."

As tough and overwhelming as the icefall was, we were as ready for it as we could have been. Several weeks before we stepped off for Nepal and the deadly icefall, we had set up a section of ladders to practice on in Erik's backyard. We elevated the ladders on cement blocks and fixed some hand ropes to simulate the entire experience. There we were, in Golden, Colorado, wearing our massive big-mountain boots, shorts, and T-shirts, tiptoeing across the ladders. We were keenly aware that as silly as we must have appeared, the front-end training would introduce us to the unique experience of walking across ladders with mountain boots on. The icefall on Everest is undoubtedly the only place on the planet where that scenario would play out. We were glad we took those preparatory steps to ease the discomfort, if only a little bit.

In early 2000, I was rounding the corner on completing the final stages of my physician assistant program. My climbing career had been put on hold for two years as I battled through the toughest academic gauntlet of my life. I was living out of my truck and occasionally in med school dorms all over the Eastern Seaboard while I completed my six-week specialty rotations. That period of time is what I called my "skinny-fat" era. My mountain climbing muscles and mind that had been finely crafted after years toiling away on Denali (Mount McKinley) had withered away with cheesesteaks and beer. I was resolutely focused on being a physician assistant and was acutely aware that I was going to have to work harder than the guy next to me in my class if I wanted to see that dream materialize. But one of the sacrificial byproducts was losing my sinewy mountain climbing conditioning.

So, when my blind buddy Erik reached out to me to see if I was interested in climbing Mount Everest with him, it seemed a bit far-fetched. First of all, a blind guy on Everest? What a shit show that would be. No blind person had even had a vapor trail of a thought of climbing the highest mountain in the world. And probably for good reason. Dozens and dozens of folks with perfectly good eyesight had perished on Everest. It turns out, there are a lot of moving parts on Everest, and getting a blind guy to the top would be a Herculean task for sure.

Then there I was, my physician assistant degree only a couple of months away from completion, and my climber body and mentality far from meeting the requirements that the highest mountain in the world would mandate, especially if I was to be the primary guide for the first-ever blind attempt on Everest. To even consider this I would need to: graduate from an arduous medical program in Philadelphia, move back to Colorado, prepare for and take my medical boards, secure a tough-to-come-by ER job, train my ass off in between "new guy" shifts in the ER, probably then quit this new job, move all my stuff into storage, and then take off for Nepal. All in nine months.

Easy.

I'm in.

And so it began. I committed myself to Erik, the mountain, and my newfound profession. I ain't gonna lie; that was a hectic run for sure. Every single day was full. I was lucky if I ever got more than six hours of sleep in one spell. But I intuitively knew that this was a once in a lifetime opportunity that would require every thread of my effort. If I was going to guide Erik on Everest, the most volatile, complex, uncertain place on the planet, I would need to be at the peak of my capacities, mentally and physically. I would not only be responsible for my life, but that of my blind partner. Every step, every move, every command would be the difference between life and death. I knew this and threw myself at it with all I had.

Back in 2001, Everest looked very little like it does these days. Back then, the mountain and surrounding infrastructure was raw, to say the least. The firm grip of commercialization had yet to fully take hold of the Khumbu Valley, and climbing Everest still provided a fairly real alpine experience. The past twenty years have seen the mountain become dialed in at a high logistical level; camps are cushy (off the ground mattress beds), weather is easier to predict, food is helicoptered in, and Sherpas do even more of the work to make the climbing easier. Don't get me wrong; you still have to get your body up and down the mountain, but the bandwidth it takes is just less of a pull on every climber these days. Every subsequent year I have spent on or near Everest since our ascent in 2001 reinforces the gratitude I have that we had our monumental Everest climb prior to the commercialization that now exists on that beautiful hill.

When we climb these big peaks that crest over the critical height of 8,000 meters (26,000 feet), we rely heavily on remote meteorologists for accurate weather forecasts. Since the well-documented debacle that took place in 1996 (Jon Krakauer's *Into Thin Air*), the ability to identify big storm systems has become commonplace. Forecasting models are more sophisticated now and can essentially preclude any big surprise storm systems from happening like it did on that fateful summit attempt in 1996, where eight people were killed over the course of two days due to a surprise storm. By the time we entered the 2000s, forecasting was pretty reliable but still not even close to where it is today. Back in 2001, we would put a call out to our hired weatherman in Denver on a weekly basis to get the download on which days were "go days" and which days were "no go days." We would trust this weather fellow implicitly—with our lives.

This trust was put to the test during one of our trips up the Lhotse face, a daunting 2,000-foot ice and snow face. I was slowly kicking my crampons up the glassy wall of ice just above 23,000 feet in what appeared to be relatively pleasant weather conditions. The sun was shining brightly, reflecting off the sheer ice and creating a paradoxically searing heat accompanied by the ten degree Fahrenheit ambient temperature. Although I had my massive down suit on, the front zipper was open down to my waist. It's not often that you can drip sweat in subfreezing temps.

Erik was climbing within shouting distance behind me. Occasionally I would glance back at him, providing the necessary micro-adjustments to his path or technique as he moved up the face. Considering the scale and immensity of the terrain, we were moving along at a fairly nice clip. With every step, Erik was setting a new record for the highest elevation a blind person had ever climbed. We were climbing into the unknown, and the profundity of what we were doing was not lost on any of us. The balance of emotions seemed to flutter between anxiety, excitement, and confidence, and we were embracing every step of the journey.

We were about two-thirds of the way up the face when, as I gazed up toward the top of the Lhotse face, a dark cloud wall caught my eye. I actually stopped climbing as I took in the power and violence barreling over the summit of the 28,000-foot Lhotse. It had a menacing look to it in stark contrast to the brilliant blue sky that it was quickly consuming. I looked back at Erik, still unknowingly climbing up toward me. Within a minute, I could tell this was more than just a dark cloud. This was a full-on storm that was being pushed at high speed by the jet stream and was on track to devour us within the next twenty minutes.

But wait, this was a "go day." We had received a detailed weather forecast from our guy in Denver just the day before, and the overwhelming sentiment was that today was a good day to head up to Camp III. No need to worry about any potential storms. "The next seventy-two hours look clear as can be," he told us over the satellite phone call. Well, I'm no meteorologist, but I was quite sure we were about to get our asses handed to us at 23,000 feet by a massive storm cell.

I was pissed. All I could imagine was this well-compensated weatherman dude sitting in his cozy office with his bathrobe on, holding a warm cup of coffee with his feet kicked up on his desk, telling us today was a "go day." And here I was, punching my way up a sheer ice wall at over 7000 meters with my blind buddy right behind me and was about to directly get punched in the face with all the might and power of a Himalayan storm. Yeah, I was ticked off, and I started throwing a certified fit. Yelling out into space to no one in particular, I began hurling insults and expletives that would make Andrew Dice Clay blush. At one point, I got myself so worked up and winded I had to pause and take a few deep breaths. I yelled back at Erik to batten down the hatches and prepare for a butt whooping. It was at that instant that I looked back at Erik, who was staring up at me, listening to my tirade with a complex facial expression that contained both fear and concern. I was immediately flooded with embarrassment and shame at how I was reacting to this situation. Not my proudest moment.

Erik relied on me profoundly not only for my technical climbing skills, but also, more importantly, for my ability to guide him in challenging situations. His emotional status was directly related to the atmosphere I created around him. He looked to me as a determining factor on whether he should be scared, engaged, relaxed, or jovial at any moment, but more acutely when he knew the stakes were higher. So here I was throwing a temper tantrum about a storm that was descending on us no matter how many curse words I threw out, and I could tell Erik was justifiably worried.

That moment was a game changer for me.

As a leader, the onus is on you to provide balanced and centered guidance to those under your command (or subordinates). Your people are watching you. You are their thermometer. As a teammate, your colleagues might be looking squarely at you to decide whether they should be concerned or not, whether they should panic or not, or whether they should trust you and charge into the objective with guns blazing. So, no matter where you are on your "rope team," it's always important to remain a beacon of light when you're climbing through storms. Folks are looking for humble confidence, not overt cockiness. A leader must balance that recipe of compassion, self-assurance, and communication in order to leave their partners with a sense of calm and composure, knowing the mission will stay on track.

Weeks in Nepal passed and turned into months. We completed circuits up and down the mountain, carrying gear for the upper camps and, at the same time, preparing our bodies for the deadly, hypoxic (lack of oxygen) way of life above 26,000 feet. Every trip up through the icefall also had the adjunct effect of improving our critical communication skills. This was such unique terrain that required absolute precise direction but not at the expense of gassing me in a short spell. In an effort to conserve my energy and not overload him with information, I had to provide Erik only the beta he needed and nothing more. I couldn't waste a single word or a purposeless look back over my shoulder. Efficiency was paramount.

As our summit night approached, it was obvious that none of the other four teams attempting the mountain that year wanted to be anywhere close to our team on that long night where speed equals safety. They made it clear in our initial communal Base Camp meetings that they were afraid the "blind guy team" would be slow and jeopardize their speed and efficiency on the long and arduous effort of summit night. We weren't gonna hate on them for that. It just provided us more space and less crowding. The other teams agreed to bookend our summit attempt; three teams would go for their summit attempt prior to our date, and one would head out after we had come down. So theoretically, we would be all by our lonesome on the biggest night of our lives. Fast-forward a couple of decades, and we all know what a junk show Everest has become with overcrowding. Little did any of us know back then how good we had it.

All of our "rotations" were now complete. We had been up and down the lower and middle flanks of the mountain several times, through the icefall four round trips, and our bodies were as optimized for acclimatization as they would most likely get. It was time to go for it.

On the evening of May 24, our team was poised at Camp IV, which sits on the South Col at 26,000 feet. A desolate and barren location in its best light, this perch is the stepping off point for summit attempts with the kind of altitude that humbles even the strongest of climbers.

Every step Erik took up from just above Camp II (22,000 feet) was setting a new record for the highest a blind person had ever stepped (actually, he was breaking his own record from when he summited Aconcagua at 22,800 feet, a few years prior). Clearly, no playbook existed on how to guide a blind guy while climbing in the Death Zone, so we were literally making up our strategy as we went.

Our predeparture conversations on stratagem were based on our experiences with all of the variables over which we had some influence: terrain, altitude, Erik's skill set, and our ability to give him verbal instructions with oxygen masks on, to name a few. Then there were the variants that we had little control over, namely: the weather and how our bodies would subjectively respond to the extreme altitude. We committed to making decisions based on evidence and real-time conditions. Our approach would inherently avoid recklessness and emotionally driven decisions. We knew this would have to be our recipe;

otherwise, we would crumble with summit fever and make rash judgment calls.

Including our Sherpas, we were a team of twenty, all huddled up in a "circle the wagons" tent assembly. The tents were faced in like wheel spokes so we could pass food and melted snow, and have logistical discussions above the blowing gale. We would have a few hours to rest in our tents that evening, with the caveat being that we were positioned smack dab in the middle of a jet stream wind tunnel, catching the full brunt of the fifty mile per hour gusts, not exactly pleasant napping weather. But when the alarm went off at eight p.m., I realized that I had actually dozed off for a solid spell and felt fairly rested, all things considered.

Stepping off into the unknown darkness that night was as an ethereal experience as I have ever encountered. I do believe we all understood the gravitas of what we were embarking on but still saw it through the lens of innocence. We were just a group of friends taking our blind buddy out for another summit attempt, just like we'd done dozens and dozens of times before. I'm still convinced that the way we perceived it as "just another summit" allowed us to maintain a sense of calm and focus that we might have lost if we would have allowed the fear of taking the first blind guy to the top of the world to live inside our heads.

The first significant landmark on summit night is a spot called the Balcony, which sits at 27,500 feet. It was still dark with a minus-ten degree Fahrenheit wind blowing onto the right side of our cheeks from Tibet. For the four hours leading up to the Balcony, my entire world was narrowed down into a twenty-foot beam of light cast from my headlamp to just in front of my feet. Other than the wind and some occasional chatter on the radio, I was silent in my own head—one step, two deep breaths, one step, two breaths, over and over and over.

A quick team huddle up at the Balcony confirmed the chatter that I thought I had heard over the radio. Our expedition leader, PV, had turned around an hour before due to fatigue. That came as a bit of a surprise as PV was legendarily strong and had summited Everest just two years prior. But weird shit happens on summit night, and this would only be our first hurdle to overcome. He assured all of us that he was okay, just not up to the task that night and felt the team was best served if he went back down to Camp IV and helped facilitate any issues over the radio.

Several hours above the Balcony is a fairly innocuous rock outcropping that is the designated oxygen cylinder depot/swap-out location. A week prior, several of our Sherpas had dropped a dozen or so oxygen cylinders at this point, so that on summit night we could swap our empty cylinders for fresh bottles that would theoretically take us to the top and back down to Camp IV. I pulled up to the O^2 station well ahead of most of the team, with the only two people within an hour of my location being our filmmaker, Michael Brown, and an unknown Sherpa. Michael and I started uncovering two fresh O^2 bottles and began the change out. As I was threading the female end of my O^2 regulator onto the male end of the oxygen bottle, a sudden burst of precious oxygen blasted out of the fresh bottle. I unscrewed the regulator and tried again. Same result. I tried another oxygen bottle thinking I had strip-threaded the bottle. Same result. Even in my hypoxic mind, I quickly realized that I had stripped the threads on my regulator.

Uh oh. This was a problem.

A couple of minutes into this sequence of events, I remember Michael saying something like…

"Bro, your lips are turning blue."

There are a few freaks of nature out there who climb Everest without supplemental O^2. I'm not one of them. But one of the upsides of not using oxygen is that you never run out. Being on supplemental oxygen at extreme altitudes and then suddenly not is an almost certain death sentence. Your body adjusts to the steady stream of O^2, and, once it runs out, the collapse is quick and succinct. Michael knew I was in trouble, understanding that I needed a new regulator, promptly. He got on the radio to PV, who had just arrived back down at Camp IV and threw out the Hail Mary.

"Hey PV, Jeff has a faulty regulator and is in pretty dire need of a replacement. I know it's doubtful, but are you aware of anyone up here that may be carrying an extra?" Michael squawked into the radio.

A couple of seconds later, PV's voice came over the radio, "Hey Mike, the only extra regulator that I am aware of is in Ang Pasang's pack. Good luck finding him though…no idea where he would be."

There was only one person even remotely close to Michael and me. We looked over at the Sherpa in the yellow down suit standing just ten feet to our left, unclear whom exactly it was.

"Ang Pasang?" Michael inquisitively yelled out.

"Yes, sir?" replied the yellow-suited man.

"Do you have an extra regulator in your pack?" I asked.

Without a word, Ang Pasang took off his pack and opened the top. The first item he pulled out was a fresh, beautiful regulator mask.

I think Michael and I both let out a perfectly synchronized, "Well, holy shit."

I VERY carefully threaded the new regulator onto the fresh cylinder and took a big draw, instantly feeling the resurgence of strength flow through my body and brain.

Sometimes you've got no other option but to rely on your teammates to pull you out of chaos. You've arrived at this juncture and are either helpless to correct the problem or perhaps a teammate is more capable of righting the ship than you are. Michael remained calm and levelheaded in the face of a life-threatening situation. Trusting your squad's inherent skills is essential, all the while knowing that undoubtedly you will be there to return the favor in the not-so-distant future. Add to that a little sprinkle of fortunate timing and luck, and the recipe is complete.

And hey, sometimes it's better to be lucky than good.

Feeling rejuvenated with my new flow of oxygen, I took off uphill, eventually leaving Michael and Ang Pasang behind. I felt strong and ready for the terrain above. Before I realized it, I was at least an hour above my buddies, and at that moment, at around 28,500 feet, I was standing higher than any other human being on the planet. The dark felt cold. It felt like I was on the edge of space. Breathing through my oxygen mask made me sound like Darth Vader, and I'm sure I may have uttered the highest ever, "Luke, I am your fatha."

For several hours of climbing, I had been following the nylon rope that was secured into the snow and ice, not for the purpose of knowing which way to go (it was pretty obvious with a 10,000-foot drop to the right and a 6,000-foot drop to the left), but, more importantly, I was ensuring the rope was in place for later in the day and the pending descent that undoubtedly would be a storm-riddled, poor visibility effort. I knew that the descent would be the most dangerous part of our attempt, so it would be crucial to have a rope to hold on to when we were absolutely exhausted with potentially marginal visibility. The rope had been placed there a week before by a team of Sherpas whose exclusive job it was to secure the rope up the route, essentially all the way up to the summit. I had been following this rope without any issue until it suddenly just ended.

I remember uttering a, "What the hell?"

But after a wider look, I realized the rope split off into two options. I could see that one version went off forty or fifty feet to my left then took a sudden turn straight up the slope through what appeared to be hundreds of feet of broken up, shaley rock, concluding at the South Summit (still a couple of hours from the true summit). The kind of terrain that Erik absolutely hates. This is the kind of topography where he slaps a foot up, only to have it slowly slide back down in the loose rubble. It was the prototypical "two steps up, one step down" syndrome. I had seen it happen with Erik on this type of ground on mountains all over the world. I knew that if I followed the rope up that way it would break Erik off, and potentially sap all the strength he would need to summit and get back down.

Alternatively, I noticed that a different rope continued straight up the snowy slope in front of us for several hundred feet, up to the same end point as the "rocky rope." It was secured to the same slope we had been climbing up, perfect sixty-degree snow and ice, the type of terrain Erik (and the rest of us) really enjoy. The only issue was that it appeared to be buried under what looked to be at least a foot, maybe two feet of that same packed snow and ice. I quickly surmised that if I intended to keep us on track with this "easier" terrain and avoid the loose rocks, I would have to dig the buried rope out from its icy confinement. It wasn't a mystery…digging ropes out at 28,500 feet would sap any remaining juice I had in the tank and mean my summit bid would be over. One of my teammates, Brad, was closing in on me as I was encountering this issue and quickly realized what we had in store.

"Looks like we're at a bit of a crossroads," Brad said.

"It does appear that way," I uttered.

Now I didn't know it then, but I sure know it now in my rearview mirror:

That was one of the greatest moments of my life. It was my moment to decide who I wanted to be, as a teammate, as a leader, as a brother, as a human being.

You can define leadership a thousand different ways. Each of us has our own personalized methods and strategies for being an effective leader. Hell, you can go to Barnes & Noble and head over to their leadership section and pull down any one of the hundred leadership books. They all have something powerful and useful. Some are better than others, but all have some element that resonates with us as we try to develop into being better leaders in times of uncertainty. Although my definition of effective leadership is broad and inclusive of many attributes, when I distill it all down to its simplest form, I feel effective leadership requires a leader to do less talking and more walking. It's seeking out opportunities to show your team your level of commitment. Leading by example and not shying away from charging into and through the complex landscapes.

So, I started digging with Brad right behind, and with him taking a turn up front from time to time.

We dug at that stinkin' rope for two hours. Chop with the ice axe, pull a couple of feet of rope out, take a few steps up. Chop, pull, step, repeat. Over and over and over. Big blocks of snow and ice would fall down the slope beneath my feet with every pull. I knew this was my mission for that morning, and so be it. I poured myself into it with every ounce of feeble strength I could muster—for two hours.

And then, with one final yank, I pulled the rope until it went banjo-string tight, freeing the last remaining bit leading up to the South Summit. From there I got my first close-up view of the Southeast Ridge that led across to the Hillary Step and, then ultimately, the top of the world. It was a daunting stretch of earth with massive exposure on both sides of the ridge. Clearly, this was "don't screw the pooch" terrain.

Only a couple of minutes after arriving onto the South Summit, my teammates began pulling into the same small mound of ice. One by one, we all hugged and high-fived, knowing that the summit was within grasp. At the end of the queue was Erik, who methodically made his way up to me, taking in big, deep breaths before hugging me and blurting out,

"Dude, I'd ask you what you've been doing for the past couple hours, but since I've been gettin' pelted by snow and ice, I've got a pretty good idea. Thanks for doing that bro. Now, let's go knock this thing off."

I had already done a physical inventory, and, just as anticipated, I was gassed. I figured I had enough juice to get to the top, but what was unclear was whether I had enough to then get back down. I wanted to remain an asset to the team and not become a liability. If I got so fatigued that I needed assistance on the descent, I'd end up being an energy suck on my teammates, who were all pushing the ends of their own exhaustion envelopes.

"I'm smoked bro…probably gonna have to call it good here," I told Erik.

Erik shook his head in disbelief. "Say what?" he said.

A few weeks later, in Kathmandu, Erik confided to me that in that moment on the South Summit, when I told him I would most likely not join him climbing to the top, he nearly called it quits himself. He knew all too well that every significant summit he had ever stood on, I had been right next to him. And here was the biggest one of all, and he knew exactly how it had gone down.

Then he inquired, "Well…if you go down, what do you think I should do?"

"Go finish this thing, Bro," I replied.

We leaned towards each other and shared a heartfelt hug. I felt a little tear drop down under my O^2 mask, hit the sub-zero-degree air, and immediately freeze to my cheek. As Erik pulled away, I could see his tears and snot had frozen under his mask as well. Our teammate Luis prompted Erik to fall in behind him, rappel down the South Summit, and begin the precarious traverse over to the Hillary Step.

I wasn't sad. I wasn't disappointed. In fact, my heart was full. I was proud as I watched my best friend, who happened to be blind, proceed on to the final ridge toward the top of the planet. It was clear to me that, at some point over the course of our two-month expedition, every single teammate had gone above and beyond what was expected of them. Every individual had shelved their own agenda and done everything in their power to propel the team upward. Whether it was making an extra trip through the icefall, carrying a heavier pack, or taking a long shift guiding Erik, each man had been there for the others, all knowing and embracing the axiom that at times, when the call is there, you step up and provide aid to your teammates. Michael and Ang Pasang did it for me when I was in need. Brad and I did it for Erik and the team when they were in need. Adversity can splinter unconsolidated groups. It can fracture an otherwise cohesive unit. But when that team is truly committed to each other in a strong and selfless way, the adversity becomes fuel and an opportunity to thrive and grow.

As I was kneeling down and watching Luis and Erik lower off the South Summit and start heading over to the real summit, it was clear that I would never be able to repeat this opportunity with Erik. This was a once in a lifetime event, and if I was ever going to dig down to the absolute reserves of my energy storage, this was the time. I was for sure beat down and was close to pulling a Jackson Browne (aka "Runnin' On Empty"), but I've known for years that we always have way more in the tank than we think. We are all capable of going beyond that glowing gas pump warning light that comes on in your vehicle. It's possible to get deeper, and I knew it, and this was my chance to go there.

I took a big breath, lowered off the South Summit, and slid in right behind Erik and Luis, carefully placing each step, one in front of the other, knowing the consequences were dire with even the smallest mistake. Up and over the legendary Hillary Step, and then, after two hours on the ridge, finally pulling up and onto the top of the Earth.

We hugged. We cried. We laughed. We breathed deeply.

We did it. We defied conventional wisdom and got the first blind man to the top of Mount Everest.

As we all commented on the profound beauty from our high perch and how we could see the curvature of the Earth, Erik pulled out perhaps the best line in the history of blind jokes,

"Hey guys, I know it's just my gig, but this view is just overrated as hell."

That got us all belly laughing just prior to turning toward the most dangerous part of the entire day. The descent.

It turns out I did have enough juice to get back down. We all fell into our tents back at Camp IV after nineteen to twenty hours of solid movement. We were collectively tired as hell, but the level of satisfaction and pride was evident. Everyone was safe, and we had done it.

Once we got back down to Base Camp, we realized we had done a few notable things. We got the first blind guy to the summit of the world. Pretty confident that that record will never be broken. As far as I can tell, there are no other blind dudes dumb enough to try and replicate Erik's feat. But the record we were the proudest of, every one of us, was that including our Sherpas, we had nineteen climbers summit from one team on the same day. The previous record was ten. I can't see how that record will ever be broken with the current situation on Everest. The commercialization of the biggest mountain in the world has been well-documented recently, and the "dilution of the team" has become apparent. Now you have countless deep-pocketed clients paying upwards of $100,000 for their opportunity to summit the highest mountain in the world. They meet their "teammates" in Kathmandu just prior to stepping off on a very dangerous objective, and then, when the shit hits the fan, it dissolves into an "every man/woman for themselves" agenda. The guides and Sherpas have their hands full as they become the only ones on the hill who have an optic based on working for others before themselves. This is exactly why so many stories become so front and center every spring as the Everest season ramps up. Our team was in it for something bigger than any one of us individually, a selfless, shared, end objective, and it was notable. Nineteen from one team in one day.

From the inception of this expedition, our team was loaded down with a heavy dose of VUCA. It seemed at every turn we were provided another shitshow to manage. But what did we think we would encounter taking a blind guy up on the biggest mountain on the planet? We asked for it. And we got it. A jacked-up, steroid-laden, cross section of life.

I can see now in deep reflection that this Everest expedition would become my personal test case for the ingredients and strategies necessary for a team to effectively manage volatility, uncertainty, complexity, and ambiguity. We sought it out and accepted it as a challenge. We interpreted each step with Erik as another opportunity to take it, interpret it, manifest it, and charge forward, not with reckless abandon but instead with calculated and calm fortitude. We committed to figuring it out and making it happen.

Jeff guiding Erik through the VUCA maze on Everest.

Chapter 4: The Earth Shook

*"The best way to find yourself is to lose
yourself in the service of others."*

— **Mahatma Gandhi**

The young Nepali boy couldn't have been more than eleven years old, around the same age as my son, Jace. His face was dirty, with tear streaks running down both cheeks. His clothes were tattered and would have fit more appropriately on a kid a year younger. He was shoeless and was being physically carried towards our makeshift clinic by what looked to be his older sister and brother. At first, I couldn't determine why he wasn't walking under his own power, but then I got a look at his left ankle. It was angulated laterally in an unnatural way with dried blood caked down his foot. From ten feet away, it was easy to determine that his ankle was at the least dislocated, perhaps broken. I could see the look of fear and pain on his face. His ankle injury would surely test our ability to be resourceful and focus on the things we had and not the things we didn't have.

I had no X-ray machine.

I had no plaster for casting.

I had no boot or splint.

But I did have twenty years of emergency room experience, a fairly well-developed "MacGyver" attitude, and some raw materials to work with.

A powerfully destructive earthquake had shaken Nepal to its core ten days prior to me encountering this young boy. Through a translator, I learned that the kid's name was Kumar, and he was playing just outside of his family's stone home when the quake hit. As his house began to crumble to the ground, a large rock from his house's upper reaches struck him in the foot. He struggled out from under the rock and crawled away from the pile. We would later learn that his mother and father were in the structure when it collapsed. He and his two siblings were now orphaned.

The first order of business was to bring some normalcy to this kid's emotional status prior to inflicting pain on him as I addressed the ankle. One of our paramedics found him a new(ish) flannel shirt, and we cleaned his face and feet as best we could. Pretty sure I saw the faintest glimpse of a smile flash across his face as we all gazed at him with his new presentation.

From my exam, I determined that his ankle was dislocated but likely not broken. Without an X-ray, however, it was impossible to know for sure. Once I numbed up his ankle joint, Kumar seemed to finally relax. He barely flinched when I pulled down on his foot and realigned his ankle to its proper position. His eyes got wide as he looked down at a foot that was, for the first time in a week and a half, pointing the right direction.

After setting a fractured or dislocated extremity, it's critical to immobilize the injury. With the small amount of equipment we could bring on the helicopter, my resources were limited, to say the least.

So now it was time to improvise…

The goal was to stabilize the ankle of a teenage boy who would be walking around on uneven, rocky terrain with no subsequent follow-up. I needed to devise a splint that would hold up to the demands of a life outdoors and still keep the joint stable for long enough to heal appropriately.

After some fishing through our boxes of medical equipment, one of our paramedics mentioned in somewhat of a defeated tone that all he could find that seemed sturdy enough was a big, plastic "sharps container." The big red boxes you see mounted on hospital room walls to accept used needles and scalpels. Not exactly the type of item you would lean on for splinting material.

"Let's take a look at that thing," I hollered over at him.

We got to work cutting and chiseling the bulky box of plastic down into a perfectly sized ankle splint, complete with taped edges to make sure Kumar didn't get any abrasions on his foot or lower leg once he resumed normal eleven-year-old boy activities on the hillside. I finished off the contraption with a snugly wrapped ACE bandage to hold it all in place. Once applied, I peeked up at Kumar's face. We both looked down at the improvised splint and gave it a simultaneous nod and smile of approval. He could now resume his eleven-year-old regularly scheduled programming.

I knew something was a bit unique that spring morning in 2015 when I picked up my phone at home in Boulder and sat down with my cup of coffee. An unusually high number of texts were in the cue, waiting to be reviewed.

"Have you heard about Nepal?"

"What do you know about the quake?"

"Dude!!! Nepal is devastated."

Before I was two sips into my cup of Joe, it became clear that Nepal had experienced a massive earthquake that had left Kathmandu and its inhabitants in a pile of shattered rubble. Media sources were reporting that the epicenter was in close proximity to the densely populated capital city, and the speculation was that perhaps 10,000 people were feared dead. The physical and emotional devastation for the people of Nepal was overwhelming.

Kathmandu, like all of Nepal, was chock full of buildings that were rickety piles of concrete with no structural integrity. There were essentially no building codes, with construction consisting of brick and mortar with no rebar in ninety percent of the edifices. All of the feebly constructed buildings, all stacked on top of each other, with Nepal sitting on one of the most active plate tectonic zones on the planet, makes for a potential geomorphological shitshow.

During my dozen or so Himalayan expeditions, I had traveled extensively throughout the country of Nepal and, in doing so, had become very close to the Nepali people. Some of my dearest friends were Nepali, and with all cell towers and internet down throughout the country, there was no way for me to get a status report on anyone. The images I was seeing on news outlets were horrifically devastating: crushed buildings, people running around the city sobbing, bodies covered in dust and soot. And that was just the urban zones. I was imagining the rural areas that weren't reachable by the news coverage. I knew for a fact that all of their homes were constructed of mud and stone, without rebar or solid foundations. Just a bunch of Jenga structures all precariously balanced on the sides of hills with no road access. These rural communities would be desperate for the basics of life: food, shelter, water, and…medical care.

I knew I had to go.

I had flown into Kathmandu dozens of times prior to this trip, but upon arrival, it was clearly a different scene. I immediately noticed collapsed walls and piles of rubble in the airport lobby. There seemed to be a general layer of anxiety cast over the place, with stern expressions and distraught faces throughout. Countless international disaster teams in their fluorescent-accented outfits milled about the airport, ready to get dirty. Typically, when I arrive at that airport, I am filled with excitement and anticipation of the adventure at hand. This was not that. Thousands of people had died, and I speculated that every local in that airport was one degree of separation from a casualty.

I claimed my bags and headed over to the hotel to meet the team of nurses and medics with whom I would spend the next month. Disasters often bring out the very best in our species. I find that the folks I deploy with on disaster medicine teams are often extraordinary individuals, all wanting simply to lend a hand to those who are suffering the most. Our Nepal medical team was no exception. A group of nine nurses, three paramedics, two docs, one other PA, and me, most with experience in austere medicine, and some with experience camping/sleeping in raw environments.

After the initial meet and greet with the team and a shower to wash off two days of travel, I headed over to the helicopter service office with one of the team medics to identify the rural zones that had been hit hard by the quake but had yet to receive any medical attention. In order to create the most impact for the most hard hit communities, we would have to shuttle personnel, medical equipment, camping equipment, and enough supplies to keep our team fed and hydrated for a month. We anticipated this would require multiple round-trip helicopter flights.

For two hours, we pored over digital maps, cross-referenced available info on current teams in the field, and the downloaded details on the hardest-hit zones. We finally settled on the remote zone of a village called Dhading Besi. Although it rests up in the foothills between Kathmandu and the frequently visited Khumbu Valley (the home to Everest and many other Himalayan giants), it is only accessible by foot, horse, or helicopter. Reports we were receiving detailed mass devastation and casualties with no indication of any international medical teams in the area.

Exactly what we were hunting for.

We were "guesstimating" that we had close to three-fourths of a ton of medical and camping supplies to shuttle over to our landing zone forty-five minutes outside of Kathmandu. That, along with personnel would require a total of five helicopter round trips up to Dhading— quite a logistical feat for sure.

It was decided that I would take the initial helicopter ride up the valley to determine the exact landing zone and probable location for our makeshift clinic. I squeezed into the bird with the pilot and dozens of hard-cased boxes laden with supplies. As we lifted off from the heliport in Kathmandu, I got my first aerial view of the vast devastation that blanketed the sprawling city. Massive piles of debris scattered the landscape, interspersed with countless blue and orange conglomerate tent cities. A dusty cloud seemed to blanket the entire horizon. But as the helicopter carried us out of the city and up into the foothills of the Himalaya, the air became more translucent and the sky a pleasant shade of blue. The fog of destruction faded behind us as the hills grew in size out of the cockpit window.

After about forty-five minutes of flying, the pilot pointed out the village of Dhading in the distance, which really looked less like an inhabitable village and more like a collection of debris piles. From the left seat, I could clearly see a massive rockslide scar tearing right through the middle of the village. A couple of hundred yards to the left of the slide zone, there appeared to be a 200-square-foot wooden platform positioned on the side of the hill. Without a second of hesitation, the pilot began gingerly creeping the helicopter in for a touchdown on the old wood decking. I felt a bead of sweat form up just above my eye as we sat down with the rear skids hanging off the back of the platform. As the pilot shut down the rotors, I hopped out of the cockpit and got my first up-close look at what real rural devastation.

The landing pad we had set down on was all that was left of the local monastery. The rock walls had been shaken down the hill and just an old wooden floor remained. Tattered prayer flags were strewn around the rock piles that littered the ground. I caught one of the several pieces of paper flying around in the rotor wash and noticed that it was a page from the Buddhist book of prayers, and I reflected on how poignant it was that the prayer of a people was aimlessly blowing in the wind, circling the destruction. The pilot turned the helicopter off, and I started trekking up the hill to determine whether this location would be the spot where we would set up our clinic.

A brief walk up the hill gave the first hint that it was not. The first thing I noticed was that there was not a human in sight. The village was abandoned. Then I looked up from my position and took note of a sixty foot wide rockslide that had barreled into the village. Although I couldn't see where it started, I was guessing that it was several hundred feet high. With the constant litany of aftershocks, some of them full-blown earthquakes, I knew this slide zone was not done with its destruction. Once again, the first rule of search and rescue: don't put the rescuers in unmanageable risky scenarios. This place was not safe and would not suffice for us to set up shop.

While I was walking around, the Nepali pilot had made contact with a local who was still in Dhading. He told the pilot that the community elders had also realized that this location was unstable and picked up the entire village and moved up the hill about a mile to a safer location.

We would find hundreds of folks in a temporary settlement a short flight uphill.

Sure enough, a quick bump up the hill, and we found them. Perhaps 400 to 500 Tamang Nepalis had relocated to the top of this grassy ridge. It was an unusual sight for sure; dozens and dozens of blue and orange tarps were strung up in the trees with people scampering all around as our helicopter circled for a closer look. The previous day, the Red Cross had heli-dropped pallets of tarps to some of the hardest-hit rural communities. The resulting image was an array of blue and orange squares interspersed throughout the forest. I chuckled as I realized that it looked like a Nepali homage to the Denver Broncos.

We set the chopper down in a little clearing on the knoll of the ridge, and as I got out, at least two dozen men and children came running towards the helicopter, as is customary for folks on the ground that aren't accustomed to being around big machines with blades spinning at 460 revolutions per minute. I emphatically urged them to back away from the rotors as I walked over to what appeared to be around 400 people. A few of the young men began assisting me with unloading the initial boxes of supplies, and a couple of minutes later, the pilot peeled up and out to go pick up and transport the next round of personnel and gear.

The first few minutes were awkwardly funny as I tried to communicate with the head villagers with my broken Nepali, their broken English, and a lot of hand gesticulations. The general vibe seemed to be upbeat and happy in spite of all the recent tragedy and loss. They all seemed genuinely excited to see outside "help" and quickly began showing me their injuries and ailments. The people's excitement and relief were palpable. I could tell that, more than anything, many of the folks simply seemed comforted to know that they were not forgotten.

Hope is an underrated emotion. Without it, we crumble into absolute despair. I was keenly aware that by seeing that helicopter full of boxes and foreigners, the village became infused with the best medicine of all in times of pain—hope. They weren't clear about what was happening, but they knew we were there for them, and with that knowledge, they became healthier.

A few hours after my initial landing, we had the entire team and all our supplies on the ground, and the clinic assembly was underway. We were lucky enough to pick up a wonderful young Nepali doctor, who we referred to as Dr. Roxi, in Kathmandu. She was just beginning her residency and was willing to put her training on hold in order to help her fellow countrymen. She would embed with us for the month in the field and prove to be an invaluable asset by acting both as a translator and a liaison in the few cases of critical patient transfer.

By the end of that initial day, our base camp and M.A.S.H. clinic were both established. Personally, I think our setup was the absolute perfect picture of what austere medicine looks like. We built four separate zones, all lined up sequentially to keep things operating in an orderly fashion. Each of these zones consisted of four tall posts with a tarp draped over them and secured. Under each tarp were two wooden benches, one for the provider and one for the patient. If necessary, one of the benches would suffice for a "bed," and for any case that required privacy, we would hang up a large bedsheet. The patients would start at the triage zone, after which the nurse would direct them to one of the two exam rooms. Once treated, they would head over to the fourth zone, the pharmacy, where they would pick up any required medicines. It was a thing of dirty beauty. Once the last bit of gear was organized, we sat down and took a deep breath. I tore up a dehydrated meal, and fell into my sleeping bag and into a deep sleep.

Those first few days were a blur. We treated hundreds of patients with a wide array of injuries and ailments, ranging from quake-related fractures to ancient-looking dental abscesses. Some needed immediate attention; some were in need of their first primary care checkup in sixty years. I pulled teeth (with my Leatherman tool), lanced skin abscesses, sewed up lacerations, and debrided (cleaned and removed dead tissue) week-old wounds. As a team, we were treating hundreds of patients per day. We would wake up with the sun, choke down some oatmeal and a coffee, and dive into the crowd of patients who had started to line up. Occasionally we'd have the opportunity to step to the side for a minute, take a seat, and eat a bag of dehydrated food. Otherwise, it was full throttle all day, every day until it was dark.

After a week or so, most of the acute, life- and limb-threatening injuries had been dealt with. So not surprisingly, soon thereafter, we began seeing a number of patients who expressed myriad non-acute symptoms that would eventually fall into the diagnosis column of anxiety/ PTSD, including tremors, inability to sleep, dizziness, and confusion. At first, we didn't connect the dots, but it soon became clear that mental health was easily the most predominant latent finding amidst all the disarray. The aftershocks and tremors were frequent and very unsettling to all of us. Although we were positioned in a relatively safe location, when the Earth shakes from side to side underneath your feet, it sends a very primal fear through your entire being. The brain has a tough time processing the fact that the dirt underneath you is not stable and is, in fact, violently quaking. When the big tremors would hit, an autonomic response would take place for all of us, Westerners and Nepalis, we would immediately reach out and grab a shoulder or hand of the person next to us. It was an emotional comfort, but it also provided a sense of stability as the Earth swayed beneath us. It was understandable after losing everything, including family members. Each significant aftershock became an emotional tremor for every Nepali on that hill. They were undoubtedly tired, scared, and sad. This manifested in the terms of PTSD. For the basic cases, we handed out Tylenol PM, and for the more profound cases, we went straight for the Valium.

It seemed to work, at least temporarily. The hope was that with time and a calm ground beneath them, this village of good folks would eventually heal and return to their normal routine of life and harmony.

We stayed on the ground in Dhading for two weeks, and then moved to another village down the valley, doing our best to care for and serve the amazingly resilient villagers there. There were tales of folks walking for three days seeking medical care from our team. We cried with them, laughed with them, and hugged them frequently. We cared for their wounds, both physical and emotional. We reminded them that they were not forgotten in their time of need and provided them perhaps the most profound of all human emotions, optimism.

I consider my time on the ground in Nepal following the earthquake an absolute gift. I was witness to the true manifestation of perseverance and enduring spirit. At even the slightest opportunity to gripe about being inconvenienced by a delayed flight or bothersome event, I simply reflect on the Tamang villagers of Dhading. Instead of dwelling on the friends, family members, and material possessions that had been lost, they consistently expressed love and gratitude for each other and what remained. These people have taught me an invaluable lesson in handling adversity—when chaos strikes; don't get caught in a downward spiral. Instead of wasting valuable time wallowing in self-pity, adjust your attitude, focusing on the positive variables within your control, and slay your dragon. They were still expressing gratitude after losing it all, and still loving each other and the blessings that still abounded around them, even after losing absolutely everything.

I'm also grateful to have been required to find work-arounds while delivering care in an austere environment. Although we had dozens of boxes of donated medicines and supplies, we were short on plenty of items that most of us were quite accustomed to. No bedside ultrasound. No casting material. No EKG machine. But when you are forced to improvise in nonnegotiable settings, it's critical to tap into that MacGyver attitude. And it's undeniable that this skill set is somewhat of a mindset. It requires an individual to embrace the WILLINGNESS to improvise and not simply tap out with the assumption that I just simply don't have the resources I need. The conviction that there is always a work-around in some form has to permeate one's consciousness. Incredible things happen when we focus on those things that we have access to and control over and stop burdening ourselves with thoughts of what we crave or don't have access to. When we fixate on the shortcomings we have in any situation, by default we create more shortcomings. When we, in fact, lean into the possibilities we have, we create more opportunities.

Consider how much bandwidth is spent fretting on the things we wish we had. The emotional and temporal vacuum that I consider the "Fret Factory" pulls from us the thing that we need the most in critical moments, our attention.

"If I only had a _____, life sure would be easier."

"If I had a _____, I would easily be able to accomplish this task."

"If my _____ was working better, things would be a lot easier."

But you don't. So, get over it and move on.

In situations where I feel I am at a limited resource crossroads, I lean on a quote from Teddy Roosevelt, which perfectly sums up the mission:

"Do what you can, with what you have, where you are."

It's a testament to resourcefulness and embracing a constructive approach toward acknowledging a void and then compensating for it. I still hold Kumar's ankle injury and subsequent splint way up there in terms of improvisational wins.

Resourcefulness is a mindset. Like any other characteristic, it is developed over time and experience. The more opportunities we face where we are forced to be innovative, the more effective we become at seeking out remedies. And, hey, I concede that it's way less stressful to encounter a problem and have exactly all the appropriate tools necessary to address the issue. But after decades of practicing medicine in wild places, I have anecdotally discovered that I actually relish the situations where I have limited assets and absolutely have to find solutions. I enjoy the act of evaluating a problem, assessing my resources, and patch-working a positive result. For sure, this was not the case early on, but now it has become my norm. By turning it into a puzzle that I am required to solve, I have "gamified" what would otherwise be a paralyzing situation. Turns out, using duct tape and baling wire to splint a broken bone can be fun.

Innovate. Adapt. Overcome.

Jeff working with what he's got in the way back hills of the Himalaya and
immobilizing Kumar's ankle with a plastic sharps container.

Chapter 5: Everest by Air

"Trust is the glue of life. It's the most essential ingredient in effective communication. It's the foundational principle that holds all relationships."

— **Steven Covey**

As I peered out the front window of the helicopter, I could see the bank of clouds powering up the valley right toward us with the look of a massive oceanic wave, a wall of thick, white whipped cream that contained enough energy to drop a helicopter out of the sky. The weather in the Himalayas is notoriously fickle. Within minutes, I have seen it go from "perfect bluebird, T-shirt weather" to "batten down the hatches, put on every stitch of clothing you have, and hang on" weather. What I saw coming toward us for sure had the look of a game changer.

Our position at Everest Base Camp (17,200 feet) was precarious at best, but absolutely necessary. The young Sherpa climber in the back of the helicopter next to me was drifting in and out of consciousness. He would come to, clutch at his chest, flail about for a minute, and then collapse back into unconsciousness. I was fairly certain that he was suffering from a condition called Prinzmetal angina. This condition occurs when the coronary arteries spasm from stress, exertion, or other factors. It's technically not a heart attack, but it sure feels like it to the patient and looks like it to the bystanders.

As I was crouching in the back of the helicopter caring for the young Sherpa, his friends, brothers, and cousins all anxiously spectated from just outside the machine, each with deep looks of concern stretched across their sunburnt faces. I'm sure they were confused as to why their otherwise healthy colleague was apparently dying right in front of them. They also seemed to understand the urgent nature of the situation and the need to get him down to a lower altitude promptly, and how challenging that seemed due to the imposing weather barreling down on us.

The weather was shutting down rapidly, and the patient was deteriorating just as quickly. The chaos wheel was spinning pretty fast at this moment, and I had a sense that things were going to get worse before they got better.

Six months prior, I had received one of those "friend of a friend" calls. My buddy explained to me that an acquaintance of his was part of a consortium of folks trying to put together the first-ever search and rescue team to operate on and around the flanks of Mount Everest. They had the budget. They had the Sherpas. They had the helicopters. The only thing they needed was a medic. This medic would have a fairly specific skill set of experiences: great familiarity with Everest and its flanks, well versed in altitude medicine, and a strong relationship with Nepal and the Nepali people. Oh, and also, this medic would need to be okay with flying around in a helicopter in the largest and most daunting mountain range in the world in ever-changing weather conditions, all the while working on critically ill and injured patients.

Check. Check. Check. Check.

What could go wrong?

I'm in.

It's become a fairly typical routine for me over the years; get an invite for some random, daunting project, deeply consider the consequences for a total of perhaps two minutes, and then sign up. I'm not sure whether that's admirable or reckless. Either way, it's this approach that regularly slaps me down right in the middle of some fairly sticky situations. Perhaps one of the strategies I have incidentally stumbled upon is that if I quickly sign on to a challenging objective, I will then be absolutely forced to immediately take the deep dive into the preparation phase prior to putting feet on the ground. Agree to go, then worry about all the training and prep after the plane tickets are bought.

Now, I had spent over a dozen seasons climbing and trekking in the Himalayas, and I had spent several seasons working search and rescue (SAR) on Denali in Alaska, but flying around plucking sick and dying people from precarious positions throughout the biggest mountain range in the world? That makes for a spicy recipe.

I spent the better part of three months prior to departure preparing for the VUCA environment I would soon be facing during the rescue season operating in the back of a helicopter. I went to my emergency department and practiced intubating and starting IVs while straddling a mannequin on a stretcher while a colleague shook the stretcher back and forth to duplicate the feel of a bumpy helicopter ride. That scene garnered some laughs from colleagues as they passed by the training room. I pored over maps and reached out to many of the guide services that would be guiding clients on Everest that season, inquiring about their climbing schedules and guides. I established relationships with the hospitals in Lukla and Kathmandu, where we would be transferring critical patients. I did as much on my end as I possibly could so that when the shit hit the fan, I would be the best version of me as possible.

Despite this preparation, I knew there would be plenty of elements that would be completely out of my control.

It's fairly common knowledge that helicopters are an effective method of transportation, especially in the "runway limited" Khumbu Valley of the Everest region. It's also fairly common knowledge that helicopters occasionally fall out of the sky, especially with the valley's fickle and powerfully changing wind and weather patterns. Storms come out of nowhere, and, when they hit, they are ferocious, slapping everything around with complete disregard.

Including hovering aircraft.

I was quite aware of these topics when I boarded my international flight for Kathmandu. I squeezed my wife and kid tightly before I left, all of us acutely aware that the unthinkable was a stark reality. One of the helicopter pilots I had flown with in Nepal during the earthquake medical mission had just recently crashed into the side of a mountain, killing everyone in the aircraft. My military friends had lost plenty of brothers in helicopter crashes. Turns out, helicopters crash.

I promised my wife and son that I would do my job to the best of my ability. I promised them I would be very situationally aware and not take any unmanageable risks. I promised them I would assess every situation and limit the amount of exposure to danger as best I could.

And therein lies the tricky part.

What might seem like a risk for one person might be a lot more manageable for someone else. My wife and I have *slightly* different levels of acceptable risk. I made my promise to those I love the most with my optic of risk management as my measure. My wife and I were quite aware that flying in the helicopter would be an integral part of this mission and that this element would be one-hundred percent out of my control. We feel better when we are in control; that much is certain. But in order for a team to run at its optimum and most efficient gear, there needs to be a level of trust in the process. There must be an understanding that each of us has a particular job, and if our rope team is constructed, developed, and nurtured with compassion and attention to detail, the ability to give our teammates the breadth to operate objectively will be part of the successfully executed process.

The young Sherpa sat up straight in the back of the helicopter, clasped at his chest, and let out an agonal cry. The benzodiazepine syringe that I was holding in my hand dropped onto the cockpit floor as his arm swung around wildly. I located the syringe, and, with the help of my Sherpa team, got his jacket sleeve pulled back to expose his deltoid. Only a couple minutes after the jab, the Valium appeared to lessen the frequency of his painful attacks. All the while, my pilot Andrew was providing me up-to-the-minute weather reports from the front seat, most of which were bleak, as the cloud bank surrounding the bird showed no indication of abating. Our flight path from Base Camp would require us to lift off from the 17,200 feet landing pad and make our way down the valley in between the gargantuan walls of Nuptse, Pumori, Lobuche, and Cholatse. The flying is precise, and being able to visually identify the flanks of these beasts is critical. I could hear the slight concern in Andrew's voice as he communicated back to me over our headsets. He knew the kid was in grave condition and needed to get down to lower elevations, and he knew that our Jet-A fuel was dwindling. He was also acutely aware of the "rule of the rescuer": do not put the aircraft or its occupants in undue danger.

Suddenly Andrew called over to me on the headset, "Doc, I see a hole and am going to see if I can get us out of here."

"We are packaged up back here ready to fly when you are," I replied.

Ten seconds later, I could hear the rotors start to spin at a more furious pace, and the turbo began to whine in anticipation of liftoff. I reached over and clipped the patient and myself into a couple of the cockpit eyebolts, the only option for security because we always remove the back seat when flying at extreme altitudes to cut down on the weight. I felt the helicopter strain to lift up in the thin air, and the nose started to point down the valley. Although I was facing backward toward the patient, I took a glance over my shoulder out the front of the helicopter and saw nothing but dense white. Andrew had made the judgment call, and although I could not make sense of how we were going to find our way through the clouds, I was confident in my teammate and his decision-making and piloting skills. Not gonna lie…my palms were sweaty, and I could feel my heart rapidly beating deep in my chest as I did my best to focus on the patient and not look out the window. After a couple of minutes of slow, tense creeping down the valley, Andrew spotted a patch of clear sky and shot right toward it. That clear air took us down to another spot of clear air and another and another until we were down somewhere around the 14,000-foot mark with nothing but clear skies out the front window. We made our way to Lukla Hospital, and within a few minutes after landing, we had the patient on a bed and hooked up to a monitor with a team of docs and nurses working on getting him stabilized. He would live to climb another day.

When a distress call would statically come over our radios, several dozen variants would come into play immediately: current weather, forecasted weather, current helicopter position, the position of the patient, condition of the patient, potential landing zone, and on and on and on. Although I would contribute to each mission discussion with the pilots, the director of operations, and the Sherpas on the ground, my job was to be the medic, not the pilot (he had his job), nor the Sherpa (he had his job). My job was very specific and had enough of its own grave decision-making moments, so I didn't spend critical time and energy contemplating the nuances of my colleague's responsibilities.

An effective team relies on the profound trust each member bestows on the others to do their job. Working on high-level teams with many moving parts requires each individual to empower those around them to optimize their performance so that you can effectively focus on your own objective.

We've all seen it, and perhaps many of us have been guilty of it—stepping out of our lane into that of our teammate/colleague in an attempt to "fix" or "adjust" their procedure, oftentimes providing unsolicited and unwarranted advice. There's a subtle distinction between lending a constructive hand to an associate when they truly need it and stepping over to micromanage their efforts. An effective and nurturing teammate will assess the situation and use a collaborative approach that leans on listening and appreciating, and transparent communication strategies. My season of SAR in Nepal surely reinforced this to me.

A week after the Base Camp rescue of the young Sherpa, the morning of May 6 dawned. The heart of the spring Himalayan climbing season was starting to kick off. Teams were all moving and shaking up their respective mountains in order to be in position for a summit attempt when the jet stream lifted around the end of the month. Knowing this would be a busy time window, our SAR team remained vigilant for the pending distress calls from Everest as well as the proximal climbing peaks in the region. Sometime in the late afternoon, we received a call that a Spanish climber was close to death at Camp II on an 8,000-meter mountain called Makalu. This beautiful but daunting mountain was a solid hour flight from our HQ over a very high mountain pass. Due to the limited daylight remaining, our options were limited to monitoring the situation and checking back in the next morning with the hope that the weather was adequate to fly and make an attempt at retrieving the climber.

I woke on the morning of May 7, and with all of the tension surrounding the pending rescue, completely forgot that it was my birthday. Our SAR headquarters in Lukla (9,600 feet) was socked in with a thick layer of cloud cover and a threat of rain. Our inquiries up the valley where our flight path would take us toward Makalu also came back with patchy clouds and variable wind gusts. Not exactly optimum bird flying weather. The status report we received that morning on the Spaniard was that he was in and out of consciousness and only moderately coherent when he was awake. The folks taking care of him relayed to us that, basically, he would be dead by day's end if not evacuated.

Anyone who has ever worked search and rescue would tell you that the first order of business is to never put the rescuer in a compromised position because by doing so, you are potentially adding to the casualty count. But this is the conundrum of working to save our fellow human beings: by pulling people out of deadly and tenuous situations, the rescuer is by default placing himself or herself in potentially harrowing scenarios. What does that risk vs. reward equation look like?

I stood on the heliport in Lukla, discussing weather and options with Captain Nischal KC, the helicopter pilot I was working with that week. He was a seasoned and gifted Nepali pilot who had logged thousands of hours flying all over the Himalaya as well as Europe and North America. The week before, in a display of skill and absolute megaballs, he landed his helicopter in the middle of the Everest icefall in order to rescue an injured climber. No pilot had ever even imagined landing a helicopter in one of the most volatile pieces of terrain on the planet. So clearly, I trusted Nischal's decision-making in regard to "go" or "no go."

Our discussion was based on available collected data. Then all of the data was weighted accordingly. The clock was ticking on this guy; another few hours and he'd be dead. The clouds were thick up the valley and behind those clouds were very large, immovable mountains. Unlike an airplane that can operate on instruments alone, visibility is paramount with a helicopter.

Our decision to go or not go was very collaborative. We both asked questions of each other. We were transparent and honest in the assessments we provided from a medical and aeronautical perspective. We had to both be all in to make it a go. After much deliberation, it was decided that we would, at the least, take off and head up the valley, with the caveat that if we encountered a situation where the soup got too thick, we would bail and return home.

Out of Lukla, the going wasn't too bad. With the cloud bank hanging high in the valley, there was a fairly clear path down deep between the cavernous mountain walls. It was when we crested over the hill into the small village of Chukhung that things got a little spicy. The wind gusts began hitting the aircraft like a rattling Mike Tyson punch, lifting and rolling us back and forth. I could feel my stomach lurch up into my chest, similar to that feeling you get on a super turbulent airplane flight, only by an order of magnitude. The cloud cover thickened to the point where Captain Nischal had to move along at a very pedestrian pace, connecting the dots of clear air.

"It's just a game of connect the dots," I said.

Nischal replied with a spry, "Yep, connect the sucker holes…with consequences."

"I can safely say that this is the most exciting birthday I have ever had," I mentioned.

"Wait…it's your birthday?" asked Nischal.

"It's May 7, right? Yep…sure enough," I said.

"Well then…we must do this extra special right," said Captain Nischal.

As we continued to fly up the valley gaining altitude, the intermittent flashes of brown terrain below us gave way to snow, and then, with a full dramatic entrance, the massive glaciated face of Imja Tse filled the entire window of the cockpit. Fluted ridges dropped thousands of feet from the summit, cresting over massive hanging glaciers, all just a few hundred feet from our helicopter. It almost felt like we could reach out and touch the mountain's flank. Nischal made a deft turn to the left to steer us away from the wall as the sky opened up before us. Just as the bird tilted to the left, Nischal's GPS iPad, which was attached to the front window via suction cup, popped off and clattered onto the cockpit floor and, to make matters worse, slid up under his seat.

Now, it's dangerous enough when this happens while you're driving down the road in your car, but dropping your handheld device under the seat while you are flying a helicopter at 19,000 feet surrounded by Himalayan giants is fairly unsettling. With the collected calm of a seasoned pilot, Nischal worked the yaw pedals and the cyclic stick gently while fishing around under his seat with his right hand, a smile across his face.

"Ah-ha!" he blurted as his right arm came up from below with the wayward iPad in hand.

I gave out a weak and ever so slightly concerned, "Oh, good."

"Doc, can you hold this for me so I can see where to go?"

As I held the GPS for Nischal to peer over at intermittently, I could see that up ahead, another cloud bank blocked what looked to be our intended path. Nischal clearly took note, and I felt the bird tilt to the left again. We began climbing even higher now, attempting to find a clear route over the pass and over to the Makalu valley. I could see on the GPS that we had just crested over 21,000 feet, tinkering close to the high-altitude range of this powerful AStar B3 machine. The thwap of the rotors took on that familiar deep sound as they tried hard to dig into the anemic air.

Then Everest came into view, commanding the skyline, her beauty and majesty belying her ferocity and deadliness. Nischal leaned the 'copter in her direction, and then it appeared: a low cut in the ridgeline with clear air. The captain aimed the bird over in that direction, and I felt myself take in a breath and hold it as we crested over the 21,200-foot ridge and quickly dropped down into the clear valley below. The flanks of Makalu came into view as we rounded a corner and then, up in the foreground, what I assumed was Camp II. As we approached, we could see dozens of individuals on the ground frantically waving their arms in our direction. Looks like we had found our guy.

Nischal gently set the helicopter down on the rocky landing zone, and I quickly hopped out to assess the patient. His name was Jesus (yep, Jesus), and he was, as advertised, barely conscious. With the help of a dozen Sherpas, we loaded Jesus into the back of the seatless helicopter cabin, and I buckled us both in for what I anticipated to be a fun reverse of the trip in.

Jesus perked up a bit when I started speaking to him in Spanish. He was coherent enough to understand me as I detailed what was about to happen: the flight path, the medicines I was about to administer, the hospital that we would reach in Lukla. He voiced understanding as we continued to gain elevation towards the daunting ridge ahead.

Nischal again repeated the flight path and dropped us down the other side, connecting the dots along the way, and eventually setting us safely down onto Lukla Hospital's landing zone. Jesus perked up quickly with the sudden drop in elevation and began conversing with me in Spanish, telling me about his family, and how this near-death event would surely be the end of his climbing career. He was effusive in his gratitude for us and the effort we had made to come retrieve him. He was keenly aware of the precarious nature of his condition and subsequent rescue.

I still hear from Jesus on a regular basis as he sends me seasonal photos of himself back in Spain with his parents and siblings. We rescued Jesus on my birthday. Pretty solid gift.

Over the course of my two-month search and rescue stint, every single day was filled with dozens of fluctuating variables, any one of which could be the singular reason a life was lost. It seemed that every day provided a new rescue scenario that carried with it myriad mind-numbing, mutating basic factors. And then the nuanced dynamics came into play: operational altitude, the potential weight of the helicopter with pilot/patient/medic, air density changes, snow conditions at the landing zone, communications, patient diagnosis and treatment, etc., etc. It's enough to make your head spin.

It's easy for any of us to become overwhelmed with how so many variables can coalesce and conspire against our best intentions. At times, it appeared as if each speed bump on our path built on the previous one until you had what feels like an insurmountable hill of problems.

In each of our rescue maneuvers that season, I had to calmly but efficiently work through an operational algorithm in my own head: focusing on the decisions that I was directly responsible for, communicating efficiently and effectively with my teammates, and then trusting them to manage their responsibilities. And all the while I was doing this, I understood that some of the factors were simply out of our direct control. It was and always will be a matter of applying my bandwidth to the issues that are mine to manage and trusting that my teammates will perform their tasks effectively.

Rarely a day passes that I don't reflect on our rescue season in the Himalayas. I think of the patients we rescued: the matriarch and grandmother of a small village that broke her back falling twenty feet out of a tree while collecting firewood. The young Tamang boy who we airlifted from a small village who had an undiagnosed bowel obstruction, the Indian woman that our Sherpas evacuated by sled down from 26,000 feet, and of course, Jesus. But mostly, I think fondly about my team of Sherpas and pilots who all were dedicated to their jobs and specific skill sets. Two months filled with close to fifty rescues, peppered with quick decisions, collaborative teamwork, complete with a fruitful lab of VUCA moments to navigate.

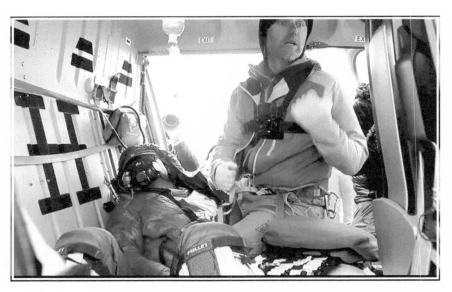

Jeff in the back of the helicopter with his Sherpa patient, managing all things VUCA.

Chapter 6: El Capitan . . . Sea of Uncertain Granite

"Some of the best lessons we ever learn are learned from past mistakes. The error of the past is the wisdom and success of the future."

— **Dale Turner**

Well into a month of training in Yosemite, you'd think we would be operating like a NASCAR pit crew. Erik, Sam, and I had been climbing essentially every day for thirty days straight. Our fingers were calloused. Our necks and arms were sun toasted. Our bodies were lean and strong. Our designated day to begin our three-day assault on the 3,000-foot face of El Capitan was only three days away.

We had decided to close out our training program with a fairly straightforward, 150-foot pitch route at the base of El Cap. We had climbed this route before, so we were confident that it would allow us to continue getting stronger but not overly tax us.

It was a bright, sunny morning as we stood at the base of the route and prepared our gear for the climb. After a month of climbing every day together, our conversation was at a minimum as I stepped off the ground and made the first few moves. Erik fed the rope up for me as I climbed higher and higher. Even with my sore fingers and arms, I enjoyed the movement across the rock, feeling the sun on my back, the birds darting around me as I made my way up foot after foot. Before too long, I was at the top of the pitch, secured an anchor, and began belaying Erik and Sam up to me, 150 feet off the ground.

Once we reached the summit, we paused for a quick high five and decided to call it a day. Mirroring our ascent, I was the first to go down, followed by Erik, and then Sam. Once I'd reached the bottom, I started to take off some of my gear and give a few verbal directions to Erik.

Soon, he had reached safety as well and was belaying Sam down, who was removing our gear from the face as he rappelled to the ground. With the day's mission firmly accomplished, I laid back into a small patch of grass, grateful for the rest.

While I was lazily dozing on and off, Erik had been doling out small rations of rope to Sam, who would remove a piece of gear and then come down another ten feet and remove another. As the anchorman holding the line, Erik was the only thing keeping Sam from falling backward. As he rappelled down lower, however, the small pile of excess rope he was feeding up to Sam was drying up. Unable to see the dwindling length on the ground, Erik fed Sam the last bit, which flew up toward the sky. Sensing a break in the rope's tension, Sam instinctively grabbed onto the gear he was removing, a split second before it was too late. Had it not held, he would have fallen backward to his death.

My eyes opened wide when I heard the rope slip. I looked over to Erik, who was feeling for the safety line that had been flung far above him, useless without the weight to anchor it. Sam looked an ashen white, hanging backward from sixty feet above. Erik continued to grasp fruitlessly into the air for the elusive rope. I sprang into action and quickly free-climbed to Sam's location with a new rope in hand, providing Sam the gear he needed to secure himself, but it was too late—the damage to our psyches had been done.

Shaken, we silently returned to our rented cabin. No one knew what to say or think. When morning came, instead of going climbing, the three of us headed to a local coffee shop. No one had fallen the day before, but they might as well have. Our confidence in each other and our team dynamic was shattered. We knew it was time for a "come to Jesus" conversation.

We had a long, heartfelt talk that lasted for hours. One by one, we weighed in. At several times during the discussion, we almost agreed to call off our attempt on El Cap, and, potentially, any future climbs as well. As my two teammates and I aired our thoughts and fears, we realized that we had some serious questions to address. Had we been lucky the year before on Denali? Were we good enough to keep going? Did we trust each other enough? Were we doing enough to stay safe? The worries and concerns that came up were all serious and legitimate. Sam wasn't sure he could still trust Erik to keep him safe. Erik wasn't sure he could still trust me to be his fail-safe. I didn't know if Sam was mentally strong enough to keep going. We were at a crossroads, and our team had to do some serious accountability unpacking if we were going to continue climbing forward together. In this case, the "C" in VUCA stood for crisis.

When we walked into that coffee shop, I wondered if we'd ever climb together again. Instead, through lots of open, healthy dialogue, truly listening to and being respectful of each other, Erik, Sam, and I recommitted to our goal and to each other and walked out stronger than we'd ever been.

In the end, we decided that we could beat El Cap, but we'd have to start taking it more seriously. This wouldn't be like anything we'd done before, and we couldn't assume that just because things had worked out for us last time, they would this time. We needed to keep a better eye on each other. There was no rest; there were no times to relax as long as any of us was in danger. Our team nearly fell that day. We narrowly escaped giving in to fear and mistrust.

If you have not yet experienced a "sky is falling" event in your career, you will, at some point. Managing a team in crisis is difficult for even the most skilled of teammates. Every time I think of such situations, I imagine that scene in the movie *Apollo 13*, when NASA controllers place all the available materials on a table to try to find a way to fix the injured spacecraft. They're sweating, under pressure, and hoping that someone on the team can come up with a solution, so they don't all die.

You don't have to be in control of a space capsule to find yourself in the midst of a crisis at the office. Rather, chaos can be triggered when you learn your software has been hacked and a quick fix needs to be developed. Perhaps you learned a product had a defect after you shipped thousands of units, and you now need to figure out what to do. Or maybe a world event has had a major impact on your firm, and you need to shore up the company to maintain stability.

In all such instances, crisis management typically follows the same four steps. First, there is the initial containment and understanding of the issue. Second, once the problem scope and scale are understood, work generally shifts toward investigating the cause of the problem. The third step uses the previous two activities as a means to outline and test theories to resolve the matter. Finally, the fourth step is to implement changes or controls for the long term.

Four steps may sound easy. However, when you are in crisis mode, there are time pressures, financial challenges, personnel impacts, and more than enough stress to go around. There will even be circumstances when you are not sure what to do. I have experienced these very unpleasant situations many more times than I wish to remember in my career, to the point where I have mapped out the common steps toward resolution. So, while there will be a sudden blizzard of panic and urgency, know that there is a solution; you need to commit to finding it.

Our successful summit the previous year (1995) on Denali had provided us a fairly hefty dose of confidence as individuals and as a team. It turns out, it was a pretty big deal to get the first blind man to the summit of North America. As a result, we had achieved some national media attention and were positioned to start picking and choosing our next objective with a much easier path for securing sponsorship. Suddenly, getting an expedition subsidized for a bunch of broke-ass climbing bums wasn't as problematic as it had been just the year prior. All of us being rock climbers first and foremost, we aimed our scopes at the quintessentially iconic El Capitan as our next target. It seemed like a good plan to spend a summer climbing rocks in the sun in comparison to the year before, freezing our nuts off in the Alaska Range. El Capitan is and always will be the litmus test for anyone who wants to consider himself or herself a bona fide climber. Our plan was to rent a cabin in West Yosemite for six weeks, and climb, train, eat, sleep, and repeat. All would culminate in a three-day ascent of El Capitan. We figured that after six weeks, we would be more than prepared for the grand monolithic challenge.

El Cap is clearly the high prize in Yosemite Valley, commanding the skyline and the attention of all who pass into the Valley. But there are literally thousands of other routes that pepper the Valley—some, crazy hard, and some, reasonable for us mere mortals. There would be no shortage of training opportunities as we built up to our final ascent.

The first week or so, we climbed countless shorter, easier routes in order to really hone our craft and become seamless with our movements, learning how to communicate without words when we would be out of sight, around a corner. We would make mistakes and then learn from them. Every moment gave us another opportunity to learn how to be better at what we were doing. Pitch after pitch, we were becoming a better version of a team. Fundamentally, we were learning how to unconditionally trust each other.

A couple of weeks into our training, we decided to step up the game a bit and shoot for a "mini big wall." We selected Middle Cathedral as the perfect trial run. It stoically sits directly across the Valley from El

Cap, and in any other setting, when it wasn't dwarfed by bigger rocks, "The Middle" would be an awe-inspiring beast.

We spent a day taking inventory of all our gear, packing our food and water, and loading the haul bags. The excitement level was high as we headed out into the early morning light towards the massive wall. The sun was just beginning to blaze down on us as we started up the first rope pitch of the route. For most mere mortals, big wall climbing is a very slow and tedious affair. Each two-hundred-foot pitch can potentially take hours. It's like digging ditches, without all the glory. But, after a significant amount of effort and sweat, you are treated with a perspective that is impossible to replicate—tremendous exposure underneath your feet with only some nylon and a few pieces of hardware connecting you to the wall.

By the time we were several hundred feet up Middle Cathedral, we were basking directly in the sun's strength. El Sol was baking us with what felt like all its might, and to make it even more painful, the heat from the granite wall was acting as a frying pan, reflecting the sun's force right back on us. All three of us had finished the individual liter bottles of water we each carried, and at one of our hanging belays (where we are all together, clipped into the same gear), it was clear we needed to tap into the gallon water jugs that were packed in our haul bags.

After hauling the one-hundred-pound bag up to our position, I clipped it to the anchor and gingerly opened up the top, expecting to easily retrieve one of our gallon jugs of water. On top were our sleeping bags, a layer lower were bags of extra clothes and sleeping pads, followed by bags of food and snacks. After a few minutes of rooting around and then ultimately feeling the bottom of the bag from the outside, it became clear that our water was perfectly situated at the bottom of our haul bags. It may sound easy to just pull items out and retrieve the water from the bottom, but with our current perch on the wall, hanging in our harnesses with no horizontal relief for hundreds of vertical feet above, it would be next to impossible.

I broke the news to Erik and Sam. Erik was already ashen white and had stopped sweating, a strong indicator of inclement heat exhaustion (which can quickly lead to heatstroke). Erik started to gag, then painfully puke up the little remaining fluid in his belly. As George Clooney's character in *O Brother, Where Art Thou?* is known to say, "We're in a tight spot."

There was no way to unpack every item, drink water, and continue on. We had royally screwed up with our packing technique. We had paid no heed to the order in which we would need to access our items, just stuffed everything right in there. Pack your metaphorical bag with some foresight, man! The analogy was not lost on us. Consider and strategize how you pack your resources prior to stepping off; otherwise, you will find yourself unable to access the critical items you need, when you need them.

We made the decision to start rappelling back down the face in search of shelter from the sun and some lukewarm water. It was a "tail between the legs" three-hour retreat back down to the ground. This whole mess up felt like an indictment not so much of our rock climbing skill set, but more so of our ability to plan and strategize how to execute our mission. However, the method that we used or didn't use to screw the pooch was irrelevant. Our operation was compromised. We blew it. The takeaway for us was to chalk this learning opportunity away for future exercises, so we didn't make the same mistake twice. Failure in itself is not a catastrophe, but failure to learn from failure definitely is. That was the last time the water got packed on the bottom of the haul bag.

The footage of Alex Honnold jamming his feet and hands into a corner crack some 2,000 feet off the ground on El Capitan—WITHOUT A ROPE—was easily the most squirmy, uncomfortable imagery I had ever seen in the world of outdoor adventure film. His monumental feat was beautifully and nervously documented in the Oscar award-winning film, *Free Solo*. If you are one of the dozen people who has not yet watched this documentary, do yourself a favor and take it in. Just make sure you have something to dry your sweaty hands off as you watch.

Prior to this monumental project, Alex was already considered to be a pioneer in the rock climbing sphere. His renown came not from his absolute prowess as the most technically gifted climber. It was more for his audacious free soloing (climbing without a rope) and speed ascents on massive walls all over the world. It showcased his unique ability to pocket fear and strike out into the vertical abyss with only his hands, feet, and finely tuned mind. His typical process would be to identify a route that fit his skill set, climb it dozens of times with ropes and a partner, and then, once all the pieces were lined up and the move sequences were memorized, he would set off on to the rock face without gear. These would be personal quests with no audiences gazing on from below. In fact, he would only share his objective with a couple of close friends in the case the unthinkable happened.

He continued ratcheting up his efforts until the obvious, yet unthinkable objective began to be an inkling in his mind of possibilities. He was starting to consider a free solo attempt up a 2,000-foot route on El Capitan.

His efforts would be the absolute embodiment of how an individual can effectively manage what on the outside appears to be an overwhelming cacophony of stress by training, preparing, and executing at the highest of levels. Although the world saw this as somewhat of a reckless act, in fact it was not. He had climbed the route dozens of times with a rope. He knew the moves forward and backward. Every single move was very calculated. From where I sit, Alex's efforts and ability to balance real-time stress and the consequences is one of the most profound displays of VUCA management in the history of mankind. It's hard to imagine another event where an individual set forth on a BHAG (Big Hairy Audacious Goal), trained and prepped until the execution was burned into his consciousness, and then executed perfection, knowing that even one small mistake would be fatal. He beautifully underscored how preparation and focus allow one to block out all of the extraneous variables that conspire to make us fall.

Although Alex's methodology and results were purely solo efforts that are tough for us mere mortals to comprehend, his practice can be applied to us all. The secret to calm and focus is knowing and preparing for the next step. Make your decision and commit to it, ignoring thoughts that aren't helpful. Focus on that next step, and you won't panic. Communicate transparently and honestly with your teammates. Voice your opinion in a level and nonthreatening way. With full attention to detail and engaged orchestration of each step, we can be fully equipped to handle even the most daunting tasks. Alex proved that in a shape-shifting way.

Preparation, training, and focus are clearly critical in the execution of massive undertakings, and, undoubtedly, Erik, Sam, and I could have done a much better job at cultivating these characteristics prior to making our final ascent up El Capitan. Over our weeks of training, we had pulled off a truly rookie packing faux pas that resulted in an aborted route attempt and cost us days of recovery, and then most profoundly, we had come within a coon's hair of dropping and killing one of our teammates. As the day prior to our big attempt drew ever so close, we weren't moving with the absolute confidence we needed to bag the first blind ascent of the massif. There were still gaps. We were still identifying opportunities to improve and dial in. Given our stumbles, we had the difficult task of regaining full trust in ourselves, each other, and the process. Having enough insight and honesty to check yourself is a true indication of team maturity. We weren't ready yet, and we knew it.

So, we delayed a few days, extending our rental house lease and shoring up our physical reserves. We committed this cushion time to polish our packing, refine our communication, and perfect our team dynamic. We spent more time on the rock and, most importantly, with each other, rehearsing our responsibilities and reestablishing our commitment to the team and the goal that lay ahead of us. Our extra days would prove to be full of absolute focus and clarity.

Then it was time. Our packing was complete—the water stowed neatly on the top of the haul bag. Our minds, bodies, and spirits were ready. The alarm had us up predawn and staring up from the bottom of El Cap by faint sunlight. I could feel my belly gurgling with excitement. Erik didn't speak a word on the walk in, unusual for him, to say the least. It didn't feel as much like nerves as it did absolute focus and determination. It felt like we were locked in.

The first step off the ground feels similar to that of shooting off into space. You know you won't touch flat earth again for days, with the knowledge that any significant screwup amongst thousands of individual moves and decisions will have a heavy toll.

We slowly inched our way up the first thousand feet, finding a deeper groove with every rope length, arriving at our determined bivouac ledge by sunset. That night, prior to laying down in our sleeping bags, still connected by the rope to the wall, Erik mentioned that he'd like to "lead a pitch" the next day. Leading a pitch translates to being the first person on the rope and placing the protection gear into the rock. By being the leader on a route, you are taking the most risk, and subsequently, the lion's share of the fear. But what comes with that higher-level risk is a fair bit more glory and satisfaction. We had trained for Erik to take that next step up, but until the moment presented itself, we didn't want to mention it and induce any unnecessary pressure. We were leaving it completely up to him to decide if and when he was ready, and it appeared he was now ready to take that challenge.

No one sleeps particularly well while wearing a harness with a rope snaking out from your waist connecting you to an anchor bolt in the wall, but I could tell Erik was a bit restless during the night, no doubt ruminating through his fresh commitment for the next day. We carefully broke camp the next morning in the predawn light with only one of us not wearing a headlamp— Erik, of course, did not need one. We were keenly aware that if Erik was leading the first pitch in the dark, it would make no difference what position the sun had in the sky. In fact, I truly believe that Erik fed off the fact that he could navigate better in the dark than any of us. This was his realm, and he would own it. Erik climbing in the dark is one of the purest examples of exploiting team assets while mitigating liabilities.

I fed the rope out to Erik as he climbed higher, out of the cone of light emanating from my headlamp, and into the dark abyss, 1000 feet above the forest floor. As twilight began to illuminate the Valley, I could faintly make out Erik, 150 feet up the perfect crack system. He had arrived at the next belay anchor and began securing the rope into the rock. Perhaps it wasn't of the same caliber as Alex climbing El Cap without a rope, but the first blind lead climb on El Cap was, in my opinion, a monumental feat of determination, preparation, and execution. In order to successfully lead climb that pitch on that iconic rock, Erik was required to hone all of the same behaviors that Alex ultimately would apply on his solo climb. Those two fellows are not so different in how they go about their business.

Once Erik secured the anchor and yelled down to us that he was safe, Sam and I committed to reciprocating Erik's trust in us. We would both be climbing and ascending ropes that Erik secured into the rock without the visual inspection of a set of eyes. One misplaced piece of gear or clipping into one of the wrong ropes (there were three of them dangling in front of him), and one or all of us would be taking a flight back to the base of the rock with a very unpleasant landing. Once again, we had trained for this. I felt confident in Erik's ability. He was keenly aware of the consequences and was lasered into his responsibilities. The only thing left to do was trust.

When Erik and I initially teamed up, it was clear that he would have to cultivate an absolute profound level of trust in me. With his life. But what is often lost in conversation when folks talk to me about the relationship that I have developed with Erik is the irrefutable level of trust I would, in turn, have to place in him. With my life. True and absolute trust has to be reciprocal and unequivocal, and it's established through sharing mutual objectives. Erik and I intuitively knew this at the outset of our relationship.

Erik pulled up the rope as I climbed up the rock, repeating his previous moves. Sam began "jugging" the other rope with the haul bag just below him (using one-way ascenders that slide up the rope but don't let you slide down). All of our weight and lives were on Erik and his anchors. The trust was palpable.

Sam and I pulled into the belay position right next to Erik and all silently hugged each other, the pride and satisfaction just oozing out of Erik, and, for that matter, all three of us. I strongly felt that Erik leading that pitch and us entrusting him with our lives would be a powerful catalyst for our team in subsequent expeditions and projects. It was a galvanizing moment that would provide us an even deeper foundation to take calculated risks that were formed on preparation, trust, and teamwork.

We had come a long way in the couple of weeks since our team was on the precipice of dismantling due to an extremely close call. Erik now knew that his boys trusted him with their lives and, therefore, could continue on as a true team of brothers. Most of the effective team leaders I am familiar with don't have the attitude of, "If I want something done right, I have to do it myself." Although it's challenging at times as a leader, we can be best served by relinquishing control and giving subordinates or team members opportunities to prove to the boss, team, and themselves that they are competent and can be trusted. Without this, your team will never truly be a cohesive team. And a loosely configured team will never be able to survive and thrive when a VUCA situation arises.

Two days later, we would top out on the summit of El Capitan, a tad bit sunburnt and maybe a little sore, but undoubtedly ecstatic. The first blind ascent of El Cap and the first blind big wall lead are both fairly monumental accomplishments. The beers flowed that night alongside the laughs and tall tales.

Our training process provided us the necessary obstacles that would require us to knuckle down and seek a deeper focus and mandatory refinement of our intentions. We had experienced adversities, learned from them, and used our screwups as feedback for improvement. We had faced a compulsory need to be the best version of a complete squad we could be. The year before, on Denali, we had established a bedrock of trust. Climbing El Capitan would prove to be the laboratory where we cemented what it meant to be a team.

More than any expedition or project I have been a part of, this one underscored how a team can effectively work through the process of "**storming, norming,** and **performing.**" Psychologist Bruce Tuckman coined the catchy phrase in his 1965 article, "*Developmental Sequence in Small Groups.*" Tuckman identifies the three stages of team development when sharing a challenging and uncertain objective and, by doing so, provides teams a template to become more effective in a shorter timeline. Sam, Erik, and I unknowingly followed the recipe to the very ingredient. We did a hefty bit of storming after the near "drop Sam" event. We then proceeded to find normalcy after a lengthy, transparent, and fairly painful dialogue. Finally, we reengaged as a team, committed ourselves to the goal, and performed at a high level. Our experience in the Valley that summer would provide an anchor point for us and all the subsequent teams we would work with from that point forward. We now understood what it meant to go through team trials, resolve the issue, and forge forward.

From Jeff's perspective, looking down on Erik, Sam, and Hans from 3,000 feet up on El Capitan.

Chapter 7: Primal Quest...The Sufferfest

"Unless you know the road you've come from,
you cannot know where you are going."

— **African proverb**

It was night and mile seven of the 485-mile adventure race. We had slept a total of thirteen hours over the past week.

Total.

Tree roots in the dirt were starting to slither and take the form of snakes in my sleep-deprived mind. My eyelids felt like they were being pulled shut by some invisible force. The four Red Bulls I had consumed over the previous few hours were no longer keeping me awake. All that was left in their wake was a case of the shakes.

But alas, I was 150 feet up a vertical cliff with my blind buddy, Erik, right next to me. We were dangling on separate ropes, me with my headlamp on my forehead, illuminating the three-foot diameter cone directly in front of me, Erik dangling in complete darkness, headlamp, unnecessary.

"Dude, make the playing field even and turn your headlamp off," Erik mumbled as he painstakingly climbed up the rope. "Deal," I said as I extinguished the light and joined him in a perfectly black abyss, dangling in thin air.

What could go wrong?

The two of us continued to use our ascenders (a piece of climbing gear that allows the user to slide up a rope and not slide back down) to climb up the rope into the darkness. Quietly, I turned my headlamp on so I could keep an eye on the situation while still playing into our "even playing field" game. I wrestled with my gear, the rope, and an overwhelming desperation to take a nap. Never in my life had I wanted to sleep so badly. The incongruity of the situation was not lost on me—profoundly wanting to take a nap while hanging on a rope a hundred feet off the ground with a blind dude suspended next to me.

While navigating my personal struggle up the rope, from time to time, I would glimpse over at Erik, who was in the middle of his own subjective brawl. Suddenly something caught my eye…his harness buckle looked strange. There seemed to be a longer than usual tail on the buckle, which, even in my sleep-deprived mind, translated to the harness not being appropriately secured. I swung a little closer to him to get a better look. Sure enough, he had not completely fed his belt into and then back out of the buckle, which is a huge "no-no" with a climbing harness. Without being double backed, the belt could easily slide through the buckle, and the harness would proceed to fall off, and, consequently, a QUICK trip down to the base of the rock, if you know what I mean. It's questionable whether the bouncing up and down on the harness would eventually pull the harness belt through the buckle or not, but I sure didn't want to take the chance and find out.

"Erik, do me a favor and swing over this way," I said.

"Dude, I'm not up for a hug right now. I just want to get up this thing," Erik replied.

I sternly stated, "I'm not asking, amigo. Swing over here. Now!"

We swayed toward each other in the dark and linked arms. I quietly took the tail of his harness and doubled it back through the buckle. I heard him grunt, knowingly uttering an approval without any words. We released our grip and swung back into our personal spaces to continue on with our Sisyphus-style struggle up the rope.

In times of absolute physical or emotional fatigue, we are clearly more vulnerable to making mistakes. And if a VUCA situation is going to arise, the chances go up by an order of magnitude when we are worn down. Each of us has, at one time or another, been so broken off with fatigue that our decision-making capacity and effectiveness is somewhat or significantly compromised. And this is, in fact, when we need to be the most vigilant. In the episode above, I was keenly aware that this was the time to be acutely heedful of our actions and movements as we navigated in this blunted state of mental aptitude.

More so than in normal operating times, our actions need to be slow and deliberate in times of fatigue. We need to "back-check" ourselves and each other often, building in redundancy when we can. When weariness begins setting in, the next level of focus needs to accompany it. I'll be the first person to admit that those are the exact times you just feel like checking out, but stepping up in the face of fatigue is easier than cleaning up the likely mess that comes from complacency and sluggishness.

Adventure racing wasn't high on my list of to-dos when I was contemplating life after summiting Mount Everest. I knew very little of the fringe multisport called The Sufferfest that was known as adventure racing until a friend of a friend approached Erik with the promise of great adventures and another version of physical and mental challenges. A typical adventure race will have you climb not one mountain, but several, paddle across rivers and occasionally through seas, connect the dots through an orientation course dispersed over miles of broken up terrain, and mountain bike hundreds of miles over dirt, pavement, and rock. And all of this is formatted with sleep being an optional luxury. Generally speaking, the more you sleep, the farther behind you get in the race, and the more likely you are to miss the time cutoffs. It all culminates in a "sufferfest" of the highest degree. Exactly the kind of adventure that Erik and I were looking for.

For our main objective, we set our sights on Primal Quest, a multi-day, multidiscipline race in the High Sierra of California, starting and ending on the banks of Lake Tahoe. The producers of the race were touting it as the "Everest" of adventure races. To complete the race, we would have to climb, hike, navigate, bike, and paddle close to 500 miles of rugged-ass alpine terrain and do it all within fairly confined cutoff points. And if you happen to miss one of these cutoff times, your race is over. We were guessing that it would take us eight or nine days to finish, and, at the most, we would be able to sneak in an hour and a half of sleep every twenty-four hours. Sounded miserably awesome.

Team fallout in the middle of an adventure race was a well-documented storyline. We heard tales of outright fistfights among teammates in the middle of an orienteering course, in the middle of the night, twenty miles from the next checkpoint. Fun times. It makes sense, though, because most humans are at their worst when they are sleep-deprived, stressed, calorically deficient, and physically hammered. The connection between the mind and body becomes tenuous at best, and we end up acting like hangry three year olds at the slightest irritation.

Undoubtedly, Erik and I were well versed in the art of suffering and staying upright in the face of exhaustion. We were quite aware from our climbing career that when you head out on a daunting objective with a new team, it behooves all parties to spend some preliminary time working together, learning to communicate and to trust each other. This was especially the case for a new team attempting a race that would throw all of the ingredients of an absolute shitshow right in our faces. But this venue would require a different degree of teamwork and empathy, and we knew it. So just as we had climbed many preliminary peaks in our preparation for El Cap and Everest, we decided it was imperative for our newly formed team to enter a shorter adventure race prior to Primal Quest. We heard chatter about a fledgling race up in Greenland. The little I knew of Greenland was that it was simply beautiful, rugged, and miserable.

Perfect.

The Arctic Team Challenge was a fairly new race trying to find popularity as a worthy adventure contest up in the rugged landscape of Greenland. It would be a good opportunity for Erik and me to work with Rob (pre cancer diagnosis) and his long time adventure racing partner Cammy, and get our first taste of hardcore adventure racing. As with most adventure races, this Greenlandic iteration would consist of miles and miles of Leif Erikson-caliber navigation across craggy landscapes, undulating glaciers, and burly mountain peaks. We would be required to interpret the established course route, shoot compass bearings connecting each of the compulsory objectives, and then travel as a team connecting each of the goals. What we would come to discover very quickly is that Greenland is one of the most rugged landscapes on the stinkin' planet.

To simply arrive at the starting line for the race was a three-day adventure on its own, consisting of planes, buses, and boats. We were traveling with our climbing, paddling, and trekking gear, along with mountain bikes (including the fifty-pound tandem), which, when all stacked together, resembled a modest-sized REI showroom floor. Albeit a little road weary, we arrived in the small Greenlandic hamlet of Tasiilaq full of excited and nervous energy. The air was cold, the locals were burly, and the terrain was daunting. Icebergs floated just off the coast like drifting ice castles and seals plopped up on the rocky shale, basking in the sun. The community of locals was brimming with excitement as all of the Lycra-clad foreigners began descending on their quaint settlement. Our "No Limits" team was the only US representative, with the other six teams hailing from the Netherlands, Germany, and Spain, and two teams from Belgium. Strangely enough, we were also the only team with a blind guy.

Now we didn't go into any of these races with false delusions that we would actually win or even place high in the finish results. In fact, we were going up against teams loaded with world-class athletes, all with years of adventuring racing experience. Between Erik and I, we had no racing acumen, very little Lycra, and only two functioning eyeballs. What we did have was two experienced teammates in Rob and Cammy, the willingness to learn, and, most importantly, the readiness to "embrace the suck." Fatigue, exhaustion, and misery are unavoidable components in this adventure racing game. Our intention throughout this new pursuit was to simply challenge ourselves and discover a new way to gauge our athletic and problem-solving capacities. Just as with mountaineering and with life in general, a systems test focused on self-inventory is imperative, consciously assessing the variables where we highlight assets and mitigate liabilities along the way.

The race kicked off with some overland trekking, climbing up and over a chain of formidable mountains, and fording multiple glacier-fed rivers, all the while navigating using an old-fashioned compass and map. Rob was the most well versed in map and compass navigation, so we had appropriately designated him as the chief route manager. I would be Erik's primary guide and focus on getting him across the variable obstacles and terrain that suited his abilities. Cammy would pull support for each of us but primarily relieve me when I was in need of a break from the exhausting task of guiding Erik. Within the first couple hours of navigation across the rugged terrain, the first holes in our team dynamic started to surface.

Rob would intently inspect the map to gauge the most direct route to our next checkpoint. Gazing down at the map, he would point to the next checkpoint and head off in a direct line of attack toward that objective. We were all taught in grade school that the shortest distance between two points is a straight line, but, oftentimes, that straight line is wrought with nearly impassable topography, especially when one of your teammates is blind. After a ten-hour day of "side hilling" loose, rocky hillsides (the kind of terrain that saps Erik's strength at a very accelerated rate), it became clear to me that we were simply electing to take routes that were a few minutes faster but at the expense of Erik's energy and effort. I had witnessed Erik take at least a dozen falls on the tough terrain, his will and effort diminishing with each mile.

The warm day soon turned into a cold night, and we were already haggard. Extreme fatigue was setting in, and the tension between us all was already notable. I didn't feel that my relationship with Rob was at a point where I could question his decision-making on route finding. He was the designated navigational leader, and I was under management, so I was keeping my opinion to myself, even as I watched the expression on Erik's face fade into frustration.

By the end of Day 4, Erik and I had had enough. We knew that the following day would be the final day of the race, and it would require a collection of all the adventure mediums in the course of a twenty-hour push. We would paddle through iceberg-filled waters, navigate through an orienteering course, climb a technical rock face, and summit three consecutive mountains. This was after four days of hard-charging with very little sleep. We were grumpy. Rob and I were fighting over the smallest issues, and that was clearly surfacing from an underlying frustration with each other, compounded by each mile. Looking back now, I am disappointed that it took us four days of brewing up the tension for us to finally address it. A healthier approach would have had us establishing a dialogue promptly as the discrepancies began to percolate to the surface.

So right before we kicked off the challenges of Day 5, I pulled Rob aside and discussed making a navigational adjustment. I proposed we establish a hybrid approach, combining the faster, more conventional "direct line of travel" with the lesser-known and slower "optimum Erik guiding technique." We discussed what this would look like, how we would share responsibilities, and, ultimately, combine forces for the betterment of the team.

To Rob's credit, he listened. We had a breakthrough and felt recharged as we headed out on the final day of racing. That last stage ended up being a twenty-hour affair, chock-full of all the burly objectives we knew were coming our way. Rob and I worked closely together in determining routes that got us to the next point quickly but chose terrain that allowed Erik to move as efficiently as possible. And even though we are at our physical worst, we had found our teamwork sweet spot, and we all actually had fun. "Type 2 fun" (Google it), of course, but fun nonetheless.

Even though, prior to starting this race, we had established a loose definition of what our individual roles and responsibilities would be, what we failed to clarify was the stylistic approaches to how we execute our jobs. The failure to define these nuances of collaboration can, in time, lead to limitations in trust, efficiency, productivity, and momentum. Prior to embarking on a fresh objective, it is critical to take a deep dive into how team assets and liabilities will be balanced, and how each team member will execute their job as it relates to the team's quiver of skill sets.

As expected, we finished dead last in the Arctic Team Challenge, and we were all right with that. We learned invaluable lessons on what this new sport would require of us as individuals and as a team. We harnessed the adversity and tension, learned from it, and ultimately turned it into efficiency and teamwork. We knew these lessons would serve us well for the ultimate challenge: Primal Quest.

"The Everest of adventure races."

"The best sufferfest known to man."

"The worst/best adventure of your life."

This is how folks were describing the upcoming iteration of Primal Quest (PQ). It was considered the ultimate adventure race, harkening back to the old days of the mothballed, international Eco Challenge series. The Eco Challenge was an annually televised race (Discovery Channel) that took place in the late 90s and early 2000s and is considered to be the genesis of reality television (little did we know). After a few years break, the race organizers decided to resuscitate the race, bringing it back exclusively to the US and televising it on CBS. The 2003 version of PQ would require 100 teams of four to cover close to 500 miles of rough and rugged terrain spanning California's Sierra Nevada range. The usual suffering modalities would be required: trail running, mountain biking, kayaking, climbing, rappelling, orienteering, and mountaineering. And all would be done while navigating under human power.

We were up and ready in Tahoe Village before the sun on Day 1 with nervous bellies and excited heads, ready for the adventure that was set before us. The initial stage would require each four-person team to break up into two, and get in fiberglass sea kayaks and paddle fifteen miles from the eastern shore of Lake Tahoe to an established check-point on the northern shore and then turn back south for another ten miles to the take out point on the western shore of the lake. The morning dawned blue, calm, and crystalline beautiful, a perfect day to paddle across the second-deepest lake in North America.

Erik and I would be in one boat, with Rob and Cammy in the second boat. Prior to the starting horn going off, we were required to carry our boats over to the shore and set them at the edge of the water in a ready position to run over to once the mass start kicked off. It was at that point that a few teams started to realize that Erik was blind and began approaching us, expressing amazement, and wishing us good luck.

"Damn bro…not sure how you're gonna get this done being blind. But good luck."

We'd feign some false confidence and express thanks for the good wishes.

The first three-hour segment, paddling north was quite enjoyable. The water was brilliant, the air was crisp, and our bodies felt good. Erik's blindness had no impact on our paddling efficiency, so we found our-selves in the middle of the 100-team pack.

Everything changed once we made the turn and headed south.

It started as a welcome, faint breeze. A couple hours later, we were in a full-blown gale. Winds were gusting upward of twenty-five miles per hour, stirring up the lake into legitimate, wide-mouthed waves. At one point, from the backseat of the boat, I watched Erik in the front seat disappear inside a wall of water, consumed by the swell. Although we had lightweight, water-resistant kayaking tops on, the constant spray of cold-as-balls water eventually created a straight-up shiver fest that had us on the edge of hypothermia. We witnessed a couple teams' boats taking on water quickly as a motorized emergency craft hustled over to scoop the racers out of the water as their boats began to sink to the bottom of the lake. We felt fortunate to pull up on the western shore completely intact, albeit shaking with a frost.

The remaining sunlight of Day 1 was chock-full of constant moving across rough topography with the occasional energy bar and Red Bull providing fuel. The dark enveloped us as we were mountain biking up some godforsaken trail, fatigue starting to mount up as muscles began cramping, and our minds started to slowly lose their sharpness. We had agreed to push through the first night without any sleep, which seemed like a solid tactical approach. It was rough but tolerable. We had all experienced twenty-four-hour pushes before (i.e., big mountain summit attempts, Burning Man, and the occasional Grateful Dead show), so the long night didn't shock our systems too dramatically. We knew the real pain would come on the fourth and fifth nights.

Rob and I were using our lessons learned from the Arctic Team race in a synergistic way. We were grooving on team route selection, and even with the fatigue mounting, our group dynamic was positive and nurturing. On our first real route-finding mission on Day 2, we 3D'd at a very high level (Deliberated, Discussed, and Determined) and actually passed several other teams. We were swapping out roles and responsibilities in an effortless manner and providing "lift ups" when we noticed someone with waning motivation.

But as pleasant as the interaction was between Rob and me, the further into the pain cave we went, and the more difficult it became to keep the team upright. Simple tasks and decisions were starting to get muddled. By Day 5, we had slept a total of nine hours, and the notorious "sleep monster" was pulling at each of us in a way that was downright painful. I had never experienced the sensation of wanting to sleep so badly that it hurt. It was clear why sleep deprivation is used as a form of torture. At one point, I watched Erik, standing upright, leaning on his trekking poles, fall sound asleep, audibly snoring. We had to regularly check ourselves and make route corrections as our orienteering skills continued to wane.

My special operator pals have spoken to me before about a technique they use to navigate terrain using a map in order to alert the team to a route-finding screwup. Prior to setting off on a mission, they would establish and mark the desired route on the map. Then, anticipating the moments when fatigue and/or oversight creeps in and the critical turns and junctions are passed by, they place a "backstop" on the map. This backstop is typically a terrain feature like a massive rock, hill, draw, or other overt natural marker. If you are traveling along and hit the backstop, you know you've gone too far, and it's time to gather up, recalibrate, and get back on route. This has proven to be an effective real-life strategy for me.

Many of the endeavors I head out on often require me to go into a fairly depleted place. Mistakes take place at a much higher frequency when we become physically, emotionally, and/or spiritually fatigued. Establishing a prearranged backstop can assuage some of the potential implosions. It has become common practice for me now to discuss with my climbing teams what types of guardrails we will implement prior to stepping off. This has also proven to be an effective strategy for many of my corporate alliances in how they practice a team approach with BHAG (Big Hairy Audacious Goal) objectives. We preestablish all the nuances of every responsibility and duty, have backstops in place for when things become fatigued, and respect the role of each team member, even when the going gets more arduous.

By the evening of Day 9, we had found our steady state. Beyond exhausted, but knowing the finish line was within grasp, we were able to tap into a reserve of gumption that perhaps we didn't know we had. We had completed 470 miles of some of the most challenging terrain we could possibly encounter, WITH A BLIND GUY, and we were still smiling, in between micro naps and Red Bulls (yeah, I know Red

Bulls aren't the ideal choice when it comes to amplifying energy on a long-term basis, but that's all I could get my hands on). At this point in the race, at least half the teams had dropped out due to injuries, excessive fatigue, and even irreversible arguments. With one more challenge remaining, there were only forty-nine teams remaining. Forty-seven of them had already crossed the finish line (the top ten teams had finished in five days), so there were only two teams still left out on the course, and we were one of them. It was midnight as we loaded up the same style kayaks we had used on Day 1 and began to paddle into the darkness over to the opposite bank of the lake toward the faint lights at the finish line. We strongly felt that although first place was well out of sight, we would fight like hell to not finish last. The only way to keep that from happening was to cross the finish line in front of the only remaining team on the course, and we were told they were twenty minutes behind us, and closing quickly.

I'm fairly certain that no other group of individuals have ever poured so much of themselves into a three-hour effort to simply not finish last in a race. We willed those kayaks across that lake to the point we could barely stand up out of them and run across the finish line. We painfully stepped across the line as a handful of brave folks cheered for us that chilly, three a.m. morning. We had done it. We finished forty-eight out of one hundred teams that began the race. We learned from our previous mistakes and lack of communication to perform at an extraordinarily high level. We were very different individuals at the end of the race than we had been just ten days prior. The opportunity to solve problems, suffer together, and believe in the process gave us the chance to grow as a group of people who cared about and trusted each other.

During the Q&As following my keynote speeches, I'm often asked if I have any strategies for how to make a rope team move forward effectively when tensions and incongruent strategies exist between teammates. Clearly, it's a common challenge in the professional arena where a full spectrum of personalities are on display and required to work together. Rob and I shelved the issues we had with each other, knowing that the welfare of the team was at stake. PQ allowed us to come together in an effective and efficient way, combining forces and skill sets with the clear intention of elevating our team. We shelved our own agendas and subjective attitudes in order to distill out the best version of what we could be as a team. I'm eternally grateful for the opportunity to learn these methods in these settings.

Jeff and Erik blasting the tandem bike through the chaos.

Chapter 8: Soldiers to Summits

"Out of suffering have emerged the strongest souls; the most massive characters are seared with scars."

— **Khalil Gibran**

I could clearly see the summit from where I was standing. It looked as though it wasn't more than forty-five minutes up and around the icy bulge that loomed over us. But that remaining distance would probably prove to be too much for the two other guys on my rope. We had been moving up fairly challenging terrain for close to eight hours in the dark of night, and they were so smoked they were garbling their words and having a fairly tough time standing upright.

We were currently perched at around 20,500 feet on a hulking Himalayan peak called Lobuche. The 21,000-foot summit was tauntingly close, but the three weeks of trekking had crescendoed into our summit night push, and folks were feeling beat up. As the night ebbed into the dawn twilight, our bodies were slowing with the effort at altitude as well as eight hours of continuous climbing up rock and snow. I looked back at Steve and then, just a bit farther back on the rope, Matt. They were both leaning over onto their ice axes, fully exhausted. They had both quit talking an hour earlier. Neither seemed the least bit amused by my lame attempts at some "positive pessimisms."

"Well, fellas, it's cold out here, but at least it's windy."

Silence.

"We've been climbing a long time, but at least we're not even halfway."

Crickets.

Both of these men were straight-up warriors, having both sustained significant injuries while serving in the U.S. Army. They knew adversity and had faced it head-on. But this was a different landscape; they were in the middle of an ass-kicking, technical climb at altitude with fairly significant physical "disabilities." Shit was hard.

"I could manage these ropes a lot better if I could just see," Steve sadly stated to anyone willing to listen.

"But you can't," I bluntly replied. "So, let's do the best with what we got and get on with it."

I knew it was a callous response to someone who had recently lost his sight, but I also knew that Steve needed a reality punch in the arm. His injury was only a couple years old, and he still admittedly was in the "pity" stage of his recovery. This would prove to be a monumental exercise in the reclamation of his life, and it would not be easy.

It was time to have a legit powwow with these guys and discuss what the next several hours were going to look like. I pulled them up to me on the rope so that we were all sitting fairly close to each other. I spent the next five minutes outlining what the options looked like in both scenarios. We could continue climbing up towards the summit or, alternatively, start to descend from the current position without touching the summit.

Then came that magical moment of dialogue. Both of them started to open up about their current mental and physical states, describing that feeling of extreme pain and fatigue accompanied by the conflicting burn to continue. The fighter in both of them started to emerge from below the surface and mitigate the exhaustion that gripped them. I watched with awe as the spark that had previously been absent from their eyes slowly began to reignite.

"Let's do it," Matt said.

Followed by a "Hell, yeah," from Steve.

All right then. Let's go stand on top of this beast.

As the ten-year anniversary of standing on the summit of Everest with Erik was looming a few months away, our team was deliberating on what we could do to honor and celebrate the achievement. We threw out all kinds of ideas—attempt an unclimbed Himalayan peak, head off to some remote location and climb an obscure mountain, go sit in a lounge chair on a beach and drink beers. Any of those options sounded pretty awesome at first glance. But deep down, we knew that none of those options would fall into the spirit of whom we had become as individuals nor as a team. Since our Everest summit, we had been provided the opportunity to showcase what real teamwork looked like, what it meant to not be preoccupied with planting your own summit flag, and how teams can move more effectively upward when they are all working for something that's bigger than any one individual. We would find more fulfillment if we celebrated the anniversary of our achievement by continuing to embrace those principles. What population lives by those principals more than any? We quickly determined how to best spend our efforts on this next expedition.

Neither Erik nor I had served in the military, but both have had family members who have and several who have paid the ultimate price. We felt that we had a debt to repay, and how better to do that than to take a group of injured vets on a climbing expedition in the Himalayas, right in the shadow of Mount Everest? This is the definitive population who lives their own version of the VUCA life, both while they were active duty and then again while attempting to gain traction in the civilian world. We felt that a trip to Nepal would provide a great backdrop for acquiring the skills necessary to manage their complex, post-military lives. Little did we know that our one-off trip to climb Lobuche would go on to become one of the more successful veteran rehabilitation programs in the country.

We established the No Barriers Warriors program (www.nobarriersu-sa.org) in 2011 for injured veterans in order to provide a venue for them to embrace adversity as a team and rekindle the fellowship and camaraderie that they left behind when they were discharged from the military. The adversity we face in the mountains provides us an opportunity to dialogue the fact that life is not a flat playing field. In fact, in our everyday lives, we all metaphorically navigate within a range of mountains, full of peaks and valleys. Life does not take place on the summit. Not even close. Life actually takes place on the flanks of the mountains. It's on the sides of the mountains where the real learning takes place. That is where we make our mistakes and use our failures as feedback, so that when we are provided the opportunity to stand on top of these precious "summits," we are more capable, and we are ready to appreciate and comprehend the power that exists there.

Steve Baskis was sixteen years old and living in Long Island, NY, with his parents when September 11 left a mark on all of us, but it burned deeply into the consciousness of a young Steve. With their proximity to New York City, his family was directly impacted by neighbors and friends who lost relatives in the attack. He stewed on this for years as his passion for school markedly waned to the point where he decided to drop out of high school. After earning his GED, he tried his luck in corporate America, working for his father's R&D company. It very quickly became clear to Steve that he was not cut out for the suit-and-tie world. He decided that he would fulfill his sense of duty and join the Army, with his sights set on ultimately training to become a Special Forces combat medic. His first deployment to Iraq was intended to be roughly sixteen months; it ended abruptly on May 13, 2008, when a roadside IED blew up his Humvee.

Steve was driving an MRAP (Mine Resistant Ambush Protected) vehicle on a side road just outside of Baghdad when a very sophisticated bomb blew up directly underneath his seat. Even though this Humvee was the $1,000,000, highly armored version of the standard truck, this particular explosive device was designed and built to inflict the maximum amount of damage. Steve took the brunt of the explosion, and once he lost consciousness, he didn't regain it until he was at the Ramstein Air Base medical facility in Germany. It was then that he realized the full extent of his injuries. Shrapnel had blown through him with great velocity and heat. His right arm was damaged badly, and there was talk of the need to amputate. Initially, he had no sensation and no movement in that arm. Another piece of shrapnel shot right through his temple, severing his optic nerve and causing immediate and irreversible blindness. He would ultimately spend a year rehabilitating at Walter Reed Army Medical Center in DC. Then it was up to him to decide how to move forward with limited use of his dominant upper extremity and, more profoundly, his blindness.

Matt Nyman was born to be a warrior. Right out of high school, Matt directed his restlessness into the Army. Fairly quickly in his initial four years of service, he was identified as being on the top of the "hard charger" curve and met the specifications for Special Operator Qualified. He knew he wouldn't be satisfied unless he reached the highest level of training, and he was willing to put in the effort and dedication needed to achieve that. After years of physical and mental training, Matt completed the Army's Operator Training Course and fulfilled his dream to become an operator for one of the most elite teams in the U.S—Delta Force.

As with all operators on the Delta teams, Matt was involved in countless covert and clandestine missions, many of which took place in the dark of night. One particular mission in Iraq would require his team to secure an HVT (High Value Target) by landing on a rooftop in a "little bird," disembark, secure the target then move down to the road for the exfiltration in a waiting Humvee. As they approached the rooftop and began to hover in the helicopter, Matt was positioned on the edge of the door opening with his feet on the landing gear step. Just prior to setting the bird down, a piece of debris flew up into the rotors of the helicopter, causing it to suddenly and violently drop onto the rooftop. Matt was thrown up in the air and into the rotors from his unsecured position. The initial impact resulted in the rotor slicing completely through his right leg. The force of that blow threw Matt thirty feet away, slamming him against a concrete wall. Once he regained consciousness, he looked down where his right leg used to be. All that remained from the knee down was the tattered remains of his pants and a lot of blood. A figurative BUCKET of blood. Without a bit of panic, all of Matt's decades of training took over: find weapon, tourniquet leg, administer morphine. Around that time, his teammates found him and realized that the mission had changed. They stabilized Matt, secured him to a tactical stretcher, and carried him down three flights of steps to the QRF (Quick Reaction Force) rescue vehicle. As they came under fire while descending the staircase, Matt fired off rounds from his seated position, protecting the team's flank despite a freshly cut off leg.

Go look up badass in the dictionary, and there you will find a picture of Matt.

Both Matt and Steve knew the risks involved when they signed on the dotted line to join the Armed Forces. But they will both tell you that they both felt they would be the ones to come out unscathed. Most of us think that tragedy typically befalls others and that we will somehow come out the other side without a scar. Then shit happens. And for many, it happens with great force and lasting consequences. Neither Matt nor Steve planned on sustaining life-altering injuries, but yet it happened. Whether they would successfully move forward with the new version of their bodies was up to them. Fortunately for all of us who know them, they chose to embrace their path and find methods to continue being the warriors they are.

As you might imagine, their road to recovery was rife with much struggle and challenge. They both will admit to fighting deep and dark bouts of depression, part of which was rooted in the fact that they both wanted to be back on the battlefield with their brothers, all the while painfully aware that by no means was that an option. They felt at times as if a massive weight was pushing down on them, and they found it easier to just sit in the dark rather than stand up and walk back in the light.

However, both men claim that there was a moment in each of their lives when an epiphany took place. It was time to stand back up. It was time to change their optic of these massive injuries from one of negativity and pain into one of resilience and forward progress. They were both introduced to the No Barriers Warriors program and were immediately intrigued. Join a team. Establish a mission. Train for that mission. Execute that mission. Sounded familiar and exactly the type of experience that would provide them the fuel for reclaiming a part of themselves that had been lost in the combat theater.

Steve and Matt, along with eight other injured veterans, would join Erik, me, and other members of our Everest team on the summit of Lobuche that fall. We laughed. We cried. We struggled, and then, ultimately, we rose above. We learned an immense amount about ourselves, and what it would take to operate at a higher frequency in this VUCA world. Among other behaviors, we distilled it down to commitment, compassion, managing stress, and establishing purpose. These takeaways provided our vets with the fuel to embrace the next set of obstacles they were bound to face.

The rope.

That sixty-meter piece of nylon that sits all neatly coiled up in my gear closet. Colorful, inanimate, maybe a little dirty. It does nothing as it just sits there and takes up space (much to the chagrin of my wife).

But then, when it's go time, and that rope gets pulled out and uncoiled, and my teammates and I clip in, it becomes more than a safety device. It transforms into a living, breathing therapist that specializes in team dynamics. It becomes the unifying instrument that allows each of the individuals clipped into it to become a part of something that is so much bigger than themselves. But for it to be an effective tool, it needs care and attention. It needs to be handled properly, used correctly, and given the attentiveness it deserves.

The tension of the rope between the climbers while traveling is critical. If it gets too tight between two climbers, the pull backward and forward is an absolute energy sap and can pull folks off their feet. Back in the day when I was guiding clients on Denali, it would often feel like I was "haulin' tuna," with the climber behind me slowing to a near crawl. That tug and pull not only is physically tougher for all involved, but it can also create a strain on the team dynamic when folks are tired and running low on bandwidth. On the other hand, when the rope tension is too loose, it can get stepped on or tripped over. And when there's a fall, the slack in the rope results in more time for the fall to accelerate. Proper tension is paramount. But it doesn't occur without attention.

Throughout our No Barriers Warriors program, we attempt to showcase the lessons we can all learn in the mountains. We reiterate to our vets that just like in the military, all worthy objectives require absolute dedication and commitment to team and self, that relationships are the foundation of how we manage success and failure, and that those relationships are based on the tension of the rope. We acknowledge that barriers will always exist, but by attacking them head-on and utilizing the proper techniques, you will not only overcome your adversity, but you will also be stronger as a result.

With great pride, Mark lowered the back of his collar to show me the new tattoo on the back of his neck. Written across the base of his bald skull in a powerfully, beautiful font was the word:

Gladiator

The ink was still fresh and the wound healing, but he couldn't wait to show it to me.

On our training trip just a few weeks before, I was so blown away by Mark's spirit and determination that I started referring to him as "Gladiator." He was a heavy-set fellow with the tough look of a Viking, a look that was made all the more dramatic by his prosthetic leg. The moniker stuck, and, very quickly, the rest of the team only referenced him as Gladiator. He loved it. So much so that he made an appointment at the local tattoo shop as soon as he got home.

Mark had spent a decade trying to find his grip since losing his leg while serving in the Army, and, not long after returning home, the rest of his body followed suit and began to break down. He gained a bunch of weight, stopped exercising, developed adult-onset diabetes, and fell into the rut of substance abuse. He followed the all-too-familiar course that so many men and women coming out of their military service have experienced: multiple surgeries, overprescribed pain meds and sleeping pills, bouts of alcoholism, and thoughts of suicide. He was looking for those things he had lost so many moons ago while serving his country. He missed the camaraderie and tough missions. He missed being in intense situations that required him to be the best version of himself. He longed to be on a team and feel fellowship again. He needed a purpose.

Mark found our program through his local Veterans Affairs office and signed up for the biggest expedition of the year in 2015. It would have us attempting the tallest mountain in Wyoming, Gannett Peak, with the hope of reaching the summit on September 11, the day that set the course for so many veterans. Ambitious, to say the least, the approach alone would require an arduous twenty-five-mile walk before the real climbing would begin. In preparation for the main expedition, the entire team of guides and veterans came together in Colorado for some preliminary technical training and, more importantly, to learn how to operate as a team. Powerful and healing stories were shared around multiple campfires, providing an opportunity for these men and women to reestablish that lost posse of fellowship.

Every day we were together as a team, I watched Mark laugh more, engage more, appreciate more. He seemed to be realizing that it was okay to acknowledge the rocky path that had taken him to his current spot, and that this was an opportunity for him to commit to climbing forward toward a more engaged future. That recognition alone was the fuel he needed. Now that Mark's emotional quotient was healing, we needed to get the physical part of his game ready and capable of handling the rigors of our upcoming ass-whooping objective.

It was clear from the outset that Mark would be significantly challenged trying to cover tough ground. Any significant walking effort from Mark was met with extreme fatigue, dizziness, and fairly dramatic blisters on his stump. As we wrapped up our initial training expedition, I laid down the gauntlet for Mark. I tasked him with putting in the training miles necessary to get his body ready for the upcoming challenge. Leading up to the final expedition, I was receiving weekly texts from Mark with photos of him sweating his ass off, hiking all around his Idaho hills. His physiotherapist was also working with him to prepare his amputated stump and fine-tune his prosthetic fit. By the time we were ready to kick off our final expedition to Gannett, Mark was ready, physically and emotionally.

Mark truly lived up to his Gladiator sobriquet on the approach. He wasn't the fastest guy, but his effort was monumental, and he quickly became the team motivator. His teammates took note of his unrelenting determination and struggle and began rallying around him, all the while finding their own extra gear. Overcoming (or watching someone overcome) adversity is contagious. When we are witness to an act of perseverance and/or extraordinary effort, we are provided a source of fuel that can be used as a team accelerant. Mark became that fuel, and I proudly watched every single individual on that team lean in and engage in a dynamic and selfless way, as well as take their own efforts to new heights.

It is important to note this dynamic in any team setting. It only takes one individual to light the team on fire. Why not let it be you? It doesn't have to be overly dramatic. You don't have to be a one-legged vet working his butt off to climb a mountain. You just have to be someone who looks for opportunities to show your team your level of commitment, despite the chaos and challenges.

Mark was whooped when we rolled into our high camp at 12,000 feet. He had expended a boatload of energy getting to this point and now a complete view of the summit lay before him. It was both daunting and exciting. We would be rising before the sun to head off toward the top, so that afternoon, we all laid flat in our sleeping bags, letting our legs (or in Mark's case, leg) rest as much as possible before we asked a lot of them again.

At five a.m., we stepped off with quiet and determined intentions. The team moved slowly but deliberately through the first obstacle—a massive talus field riddled with VW-size boulders. This would prove to be Mark's manageable nemesis. Every step would require Cirque du Soleil-type balance with fairly severe consequences. More than ever, the team rallied together in an effort to ensure Mark was able to navigate the rigorous maze. Hours later, we hit the snow, and the going got easier. We were only a couple of hours from the top. I could already feel the pride welling inside me as I imagined this group of men and women who had battled so hard, internally and externally, celebrating on top of this mountain on such a symbolic date.

I was out in front of the rope team as the snow ribbon we were climbing turned a corner up between two massive walls of rock. I followed the route around the corner and got my first look up at the bergschrund.

Well, shit. That's not good.

A bergschrund is a point where an upper glacier separates from a lower glacier, oftentimes resulting in a crevasse. It's a typical feature on big mountains, sometimes manageable and sometimes not so much. At first glance, this appeared to be of the latter version. It was massive. The gap between the two glaciers was at least twenty feet, with no apparent bridge to span the distance. I scooted up close to the edge to look down in hopes that maybe we could climb down the lower side and back up the upper wall. It was twenty feet deep with an overhanging lip on the opposing side. Both the ends of the bergschrund were walled off by sheer rock cliffs. I brought the other guides up to my position to get some extra eyes on this predicament. I was universally met with the same sounds of disbelief and disapproval. This thing was big, and there didn't seem to be any way around it, yet the summit was just an hour away. Our guide crew evaluated, discussed, and ultimately made the call. This barrier was too much for us to manage.

The symbolism was pronounced. Here we had a group of men and women who were all fighting to overcome all the physical and emotional obstacles that had been laid before them since returning to civilian life, and with the summit just in reach, a physical barrier was blocking their path forward. Active duty and veterans are drilled to train for a mission and execute it at a high level even if mind-bending challenges are set before them. They are instructed to solve problems and step over obstructions. For many, the post-military life has proven to be even more fraught with hurdles than the battlefield. And here was just another one. This was perhaps one of the most profound VUCA moments in my life, which has been filled with many. Our summit attempt was over.

I pulled the team together and laid out the situation. The other guides chimed in on the impassability set before us. The air was quiet. The mountains were still. I began to hear a soft sob. Then one of the men let out a piercing war cry, sustaining the call so that it echoed off the alpine walls. Then another yell and then another. We all began screaming with every bit of pain and frustration and love and loss that we could. All in unison. All personally feeling the cathartic nature of purging the past and embracing the future.

Once we returned back to our camp, we had an emotional debrief, with each person sharing their own anecdotal stories of chaos, uncertainty, and potential healing. We discussed what barriers mean in our lives, and how no success is final and no failure is fatal. It's having the courage to continue that matters.

As we were wrapping up our discussion, Mark stood up very slowly on his one leg, his prosthetic lying next to him stained with blood.

"Going forward, I will own my emotions and actions. I am tired of letting them own me. No unexpected barrier will dictate how I move forward. It's up to me from this point on."

Not all obstacles come to disrupt your life—some come to clear your path.

I started the No Barriers Warriors program with Erik thinking, and perhaps assuming, that I would be the sage teacher for these groups of injured veterans, imparting wisdom and dropping knowledge. In reality, I wasn't even close. It turns out, I am undoubtedly the student in our alpine rehabilitation labs. Yes, I'm the guide, and along with the other guides, we run the curriculum that is taught while on the expeditions. But in each of the dozens of programs that I have been a part of, I come away with a trove of learning points on all of the vital topics: Resilience, Recovery, Compassion, Pain, Loss, and Appreciation, and undeniably, how to operate effectively in a VUCA world. These men and women are the embodiment of how to handle adversity, rebound from chaos, and find clarity in uncertainty. We should all be so fortunate to be students in the halls of these valiant soldiers.

Jeff and the Soldiers team between valleys, on the summit

Chapter 9: Expedition Impossible

"A friend loveth at all times, and a brother is born for adversity."
— **King Solomon**

The sweat was stinging my eyes as it dripped down from my forehead. My body was exhausted, and the low-grade headache was still pressing on my temples. My legs were surging with lactic acid, and my shoulders were numb with pain from a month of carrying a backpack and a blind guy.

I was running full bore with Erik hanging on my pack as tightly as he could as we darted among the carpet stalls and narrow walkways of the Marrakech market. The locals were doing their best to avoid us as we charged along, but, inevitably, Erik would take a wide turn around a corner and clip one of the local artisans, and I would quickly follow up with an "Asf jda!" Arabic for, "I'm so sorry."

We were knee-deep into the final day of the month-long ABC network series *Expedition Impossible* with only three teams remaining in contention for a first-place finish and the grand prize of $100,000 and three new Ford Expeditions. We had survived thirty days of "blind" terrain, nine challenging stages, and an ankle fracture; the fact that we hadn't been eliminated was a surprise to many. On one side of me, I had a blind guy, and, on the other side, a guy with a broken ankle.

Just like I had planned it.

In spite of Ike's cast and "injured looking giraffe" gait, we were still one of the top teams in the competition, and actually our chances were looking pretty good. It was 1 p.m., and we had already paddled a boat across a lake, ridden a trio of massive Arabian stallions, dug through a pile of rubble, saddled up spitting camels, solved several puzzles, and were now storming through the market in search of what would turn out to be one of our last clues. Ike was doing his best to keep up with Erik and me, but his ankle in its cast was clearly wearing him down. The race rules required that the three of us stay within fifty feet of each other at all times, but our pace was sending Ike over the edge of exhaustion. Despite his discomfort, his warrior soul would not let him quit. I could see him grimace with every step as the pain shot up from his ankle and into his brain.

Four months prior, Erik and I received an email from a representative of Mark Burnett asking if we would be interested in applying as a team for an upcoming adventure race that would be reminiscent of the old Eco Challenge races that took place a decade ago. The email disclosed only a few details. It would play out like a typical adventure race with multiple disciplines. There would be thirteen teams of three with the last team to cross the finish at the end of each stage being sent home. It would be somewhere cool. It would be on national television and would be called *Expedition Impossible*. We were left to wonder about all the rest. It was, however, intriguing enough.

In case that you were unaware, Mark Burnett makes, in my humble opinion, crappy television and has done so for years. He is widely considered the godfather of reality TV with the creation of the ubiquitous *Survivor* series, among others. His TV recipe is to put a bunch of contradictory personalities in stressful situations and then let the drama unfold, not exactly the dynamic that Erik and I were seeking out at this juncture in our respective careers. We were acutely aware that placing a team in the race with a blind guy would simply check the disability box for the television producers with the assumption that we would pull in the sympathy-viewer demographic as we stumbled through the race. Our initial knee-jerk reaction was repulsion simply because we were keenly aware that the recipe was painfully predictable: the audience feels sorry for the team with the blind guy, the team with blind guy bumbles around and looks like fools, the team with blind guy loses the race early on but gets the empathy viewership Burnett is looking for. We would simply be a tool for the TV execs to get a bump in their viewership.

That would undoubtedly be the expected script.

Because being awkwardly cast on a television reality race was not extraordinarily appealing to us, we initially told Burnett that we would most likely pass. Erik and I had just completed the initial expedition for what would ultimately become the No Barriers Warriors program, and we knew that would require much of our "free time." This reality TV race would pull us away from family, work, and program development for at least a month, and the return on investment was not immediately clear.

But after a solid heart-to-heart conversation, Erik and I concluded that by not agreeing to run in this race simply because of what we might "look like" on national TV, we would be hypocrites. For years, we had been shouting out a message through our expeditions for anyone who cared to listen: take risks and disregard what conventional wisdom tells us to do.

All of that was clear, but if we opted out of at least attempting this thing simply because of a national audience "pity" optic, what kind of hypocrites would we be? We discussed what it would take to feel like we were doing this thing justice and represent ourselves with dignity. At this juncture, we actually had a respectable amount of adventure racing experience under our belts with our time in Greenland and Tahoe. Just as with those races, we weren't going to kid ourselves that we would actually win the thing, but we would at least charge hard and enjoy some good, old-fashioned suffering.

In choosing our third teammate, Erik and I didn't have to look far. We immediately knew we had already met the ideal guy just a few months prior on our Warriors expedition in Nepal. Aaron "Ike" Isaacson was a "heart-of-America badass" and former Army Ranger who, among other decorations, had received a Purple Heart after sustaining injuries during a firefight in Afghanistan. Ike had been recently and honorably discharged from the military and was hungry for his next adventure. This dude didn't have one iota of quit in him, and for being such a tough guy, was one of the easiest going fellas you would ever meet—exactly the kind of guy we would need and appreciate on a project such as this. We pitched the concept to Ike, and he immediately gave us a "Hell, yeah. I'm in!" Once our team was set, we put in a fair bit of training, formulated our preliminary strategies, and thoroughly discussed what our expectations and intentions would be.

Then it was off to Casablanca.

By the Stage 5 midway point, about half the teams had withered and been escorted to the virtual "showers," while we seemed to be just hitting our stride. We knew going into it that the more miserable it was, the better it would serve us. The three of us had spent most of our adult lives in uncomfortable and relatively austere environments, learning, and, in fact, "enjoying" the discomfort that comes with a solid adventure. After decades spent living that type of lifestyle (and in Ike's case, service), you get really good at "embracing the suck." We figured the colder, the dirtier, the shittier the food, the fewer the showers, the better off we'd be as the softer teams tapped out. And that's exactly how it played out. At the two-week halfway point, only six teams remained. We were working together seamlessly, communicating at a high level, and elevating each other when we noticed a slump in one another. It was midday of that fifth stage that something special took place. The level of trust Erik and I had been cultivating for twenty years was put on full display for the world to see.

We found ourselves running toward the front of the five-team pack on that brilliantly sunny Moroccan afternoon. Each turn was like a new, mini-adventure challenge: solving riddles, riding horses through dramatic canyons, kayaking through rapids-filled rivers. Every day was like a National Geographic magazine spread on steroids. We were loving every second of it. But as we stepped to the edge of the cliff, we knew this one was different and unique. The most recent "clue" we had received required us to scramble to the top of a rock cliff that lurched over the fast-moving Ourika River. As Ike took the first look over the edge of the precipice, I watched him give off one of those wide-eyed, head-popping forward kinds of looks.

"Wow…that's legit," I heard him mutter.

I gently stepped over to take a peek of my own over the edge of the rock face. The cliff was sheer and dropped straight down forty feet into the roiling river below. Ike was right; it was legit. At the top of the rock, there was a two-foot-high, decorative tower that held the next clue, a scroll of paper with two options written down in elaborate script:

YOU HAVE TWO OPTIONS TO GET DOWN THE RIVER:

1) CHOOSE THE LONGER BUT LESS INTENSE PATH BY WALKING BACK DOWN THE ROCK, CROSSING THE BRIDGE AND TRAVERSING THE BANK OF THE RIVER.

2) CHOOSE THE QUICKER BUT MORE INTENSE PATH…JUMP!

I leaned over to Erik and said, "I think we should jump, bro."

"How high is it?" Erik asked.

"About thirty feet," I answered.

"What??" Erik exclaimed.

"You've got it, bro. You can do this."

Ike diligently stepped to the edge of the crag and, without a second of hesitation, leaped off with perfect SEAL Team 6 form. I watched him quickly swim over to the bank and wave his hand up at me, encouraging me to take the plunge or jump. In an effort to not show any fear or give either one of us enough time to consider the many reasons to not jump, I grabbed Erik's shoulder, and we gingerly stepped over to the edge of the cliff. The instincts and trust that we had cultivated for decades on mountains all over the world quickly kicked in. I grabbed Erik's hand and counted it down.

3, 2, 1...

Reminiscent of that memorable *Butch Cassidy and the Sundance Kid* scene, we jumped: two grown men, holding hands, flying through the air. Looking back at the photo of us in midair, Erik is maintaining absolutely perfect, straight-as-a-pencil form. I, on the other hand, had my right leg shooting out to the side, free arm flailing behind me. Total rookie. Somehow, the blind guy does everything with more style.

We were both hootin' and hollerin' once we surfaced, relieved that we came out of it unscathed. I shouted over to Erik, "Hey, Holmes, you know what the best part about jumping off that forty-foot cliff was?"

"Wait. You told me it was thirty!"

"Exactly," I said.

In its truest essence, trust is expressing vulnerability. In order to fully trust, we have to submit part of ourselves to the person and/or the process. Acknowledging and respecting that vulnerability can create significant impact for all those involved. With regard to that cliff-jumping scenario, most folks typically see themselves in my role: being the guide, lending the hand, and being a source of strength in times of uncertainty. What is paramount, though, is for us to appreciate the role of Erik and what it takes for him to give his trust away. Erik and those who we lead need their guide to honor the emotional exposure it takes to step up to that cliff with the lights completely out, grab a trusted hand, and take a big plunge into the abyss.

Undoubtedly, the roles will be reversed at some point. No matter how much of a hard-charging leader we might consider ourselves to be, there will be a moment in time when each of us is required to step into Erik's shoes on the edge of that cliff. We will be required to be vulnerable and ask for help, both professionally and personally. Honoring both roles creates a healthy environment for all involved. Erik and I have always viewed trust as a reciprocal exchange. We are both keenly aware that our relationship is not exclusively based on him trusting me. It goes without saying, however, that he frequently has to trust me—with his life. That's made clear just from watching us move across terrain. And I deeply honor that vulnerability. But what is just as important to recognize is the trust I have to give back to him. We would operate in a realm of disequilibrium if our relationship was simply based on him giving everything to me and receiving nothing in return. I constantly look for ways to show him that I am willing and able to place my trust in him, to put my life in his hands, and to nurture a healthy and balanced version of teamwork in the face of adversity.

About a week prior to the final Stage 10 chaos and Ike's painful sprinting in a cast, we found ourselves in a very similar situation on Stage 7. We were running full throttle through a market after just passing through a mandatory checkpoint. As we approached our car to head off to our next objective, Ike stepped off a very average, benign curb and rolled his ankle.

So bad that I heard it pop from the other side of the car.

So bad in fact that this Kansas-born, cattle-fed, Army Ranger trundled into the car visibly contorting in pain. He grasped at his ankle and let out a low grumble of a moan.

"What's up, bro?" I asked from the back seat.

"That same ankle I broke in Afghanistan. I just rolled it, and I'm pretty sure I broke it again," Ike replied.

All I could come up with was a poorly timed, "Well, shitballs."

In spite of this new development, we continued to drive on to our next challenge, which was located at an airfield about a thirty-minute drive away. We scored Ike some ice and Ibuprofen, and I hopped up in the seat beside Ike to give the ankle a quick exam while our driver sped the Ford Expedition down the two-lane road. It was already purple, swollen, and extremely tender to the touch with a very limited range of motion. For all intents and purposes, and until an X-ray could provide conclusive evidence, it was broken.

Knowing that a broken ankle would eliminate us from contention, Ike suggested that he would just not tell any of the race organizers or production staff. He tried to convince Erik and me that he would just suck it up and hobble along for the rest of the race. He proceeded to tell us that the last time he broke this same ankle, he was on a foot patrol six miles from his Forward Operating Base in Kandahar. He limped all the way back with the help of his fellow soldiers with the ever-present threat that an ambush firefight could ignite at any minute. And if he could do that, surely he would be able to muster up the mojo to keep firing away on a made-for-TV adventure racecourse. Who were we to question him?

We arrived at the airfield, and as we rolled out of the vehicle, Ike stepped out and fell into a puddle of pain, within plain view of the race organizer and crewmembers. So much for playing it off as no big deal.

We limped over to determine what was in store for us next, realizing that Ike would have to come clean about his injury. Erik and I dropped Ike with the organizers and walked over to gather our set of instructions. We were handed a note that stated one of the team members would have to go up in a plane and do a tandem skydive, and, while floating under the canopy from 10,000 feet in the sky, identify the next clue that would be written in some fashion in a wheat field on the horizon.

Seemed vague, but okay.

Although Erik was a certified solo skydiver and way more experienced at jumping out of perfectly good airplanes than I was, he would clearly be a bit handcuffed when it came to visually identifying a clue written in a field while plummeting down from 7,000 feet above the ground. So, I was elected the de facto jumper and headed over to the flight hanger to meet my tandem plunge partner.

Somewhere between me taking off in the plane, identifying the next clue while falling back toward the Earth and ultimately landing safely, the race organizers made the proclamation that they would require Ike to be taken to a local Moroccan hospital to get X-rays of his ankle prior to us continuing with the race. Ike tried to put up a fight, showing his toughness and resiliency, but to no avail. I couldn't very well argue once I performed my own clinical exam on his ankle. It sure had the presentation of a fractured bone, and it absolutely wouldn't be worth any long-term damage just for the sake of some made-for-TV race. We were assured by the race directors that we wouldn't lose any ground in the race standings if we made the trip to the hospital, assuming we were cleared to step off from the starting line the very next morning.

A couple of hours later, I stood next to the Moroccan doctors to get our first look at the X-ray of the suspect ankle. Surprisingly, there was no blatantly obvious fracture or dislocation. There did, however, appear to be a slight hairline fracture that would undoubtedly require a cast. The local doctors noticed it as well.

Welp…that's the end of that, I assumed.

Gave it a good shot.

Put in a respectable effort.

Little did I know, but Ike was already scheming. As they were applying the plaster cast on his ankle, with solid foresight, Ike resourcefully requested that they install a rubber "heel pedestal" to help with walking. The staff at the hospital gave him a look of incredulity and then complied. The doctors begrudgingly conceded that if Ike could handle the pain, he was cleared to continue with the race. Just to showcase his freshly casted capacities for the onlooking race representative who was accompanying us, Ike confidently ran/hopped out from the hospital lobby and into the waiting vehicle, with a big smile on his face and not the slightest glimmer of discomfort. I leaned over to Erik and whispered, "We may not be out of this thing, after all."

We rolled back into camp well after dark, anticipating an early morning continuation of the competition, albeit with some new accessorizing on Ike's foot. Holding true to his word, the race director agreed that we could continue with the race, with the only caveat being that if it looked like Ike was badly hurting at any point, we would have to throw in the towel. It was obvious as the directors spoke to us about our continuation that they assumed we wouldn't get but a few hours into the next stage before we would fall apart. I knew Ike well enough that even if his foot was hanging on by a thread, he would not show pain. He is built for this, and he is stubborn as hell. So, I guess we're doing this thing.

Prior to racking out that night, the three of us huddled up to discuss our upcoming strategy with this new development. A quick inventory of our team wasn't exactly a strong confidence builder. On one side, I had a fatigued, mid-forties blind guy; on the other, a 210-pound, hard-charging former Army Ranger with a cast on his left foot.

I knew what I was getting with Erik when we signed up for this race. Over the years, he and I had successfully navigated plenty of challenging and variable terrain together. We knew the scene would not be pretty at times, and were far from speedy, but we were efficient and spirited. Our deep experiences provided us with the ability to make good decisions, communicate effectively, and not get bent when things weren't going our way. What I couldn't have forecasted was my Army Ranger teammate falling off of a curb during Stage 5 of the race and breaking his foot. The playing field had changed profoundly, and we didn't have the liberty of pushing pause. It was clear that if we wanted to keep up in the race, we would have to figure it out on the fly.

Even with all of the adversity stacked up against us, we did have one thing going for us; the three of us had collectively spent a significant amount of time navigating one shitshow after another over the years. For decades, we had each been filling our improvisational quiver with sharp arrows to fire off when things weren't panning out exactly how we had hoped. Having those experiences to pull from is empowering, to say the least. It creates a sense of calm, knowing that in spite of what's in front of us, we will somehow figure out a way forward.

We stepped up to the starting line the next morning on Stage 8, the three of us sporting a smile and a shrug of the shoulders, as if to say, "Oh, well…doesn't look good, but we're goin' for it." A couple of the remaining teams quietly seemed pleased that we were hobbled, as we would no longer pose a threat to them as the race was entering into the final stages. Very appropriately, Stage 8 was heavily loaded with difficult foot travel. Considering his hobbled status, Ike kept pace as best he could. Although we had fallen behind the remaining five teams, we were keeping just within eye distance of the pack, and as the final challenge came into view, we got sight of the only team that was still trying to work out the puzzle. Well, well, well, if we could solve this challenge and cross the line prior to them, we would stay alive another day. We hustled over, did a full inventory of the challenge, established roles and responsibilities, and began to execute. Twenty minutes later and much to the chagrin of our competitors, we figured out the answer and began to limp our way up the hill and across the finish line.

It was almost as if the universe had acknowledged our string of challenges and provided us with the opportunity to rise above them. We chose to stay true to each other and elevate each other even as things seemed bleak, and we were rewarded with the chance to stick around for another stage.

Stage 9 would play out in a very similar way. Before kicking it off, we collectively acknowledged that things were not how we had originally mapped them out, we strategized and compensated for our liabilities, and then rallied around the cause with all that we had. We made good decisions, established a slight lead ahead of the final team bringing up the rear, and then ran as hard as we could to cross the Stage 9 finish line just a few seconds from being last. We had made it to the finals. We were still in the running.

And then there were three. Three teams remained, vying for the ultimate prize. The final day, Stage 10 would consist of a sunup to sundown series of challenges that would stress even the most capable teams. We knew it would require a culmination of all of our grit and skill. Erik, Ike, and I poured everything we had into our effort. Ike was an absolute stud, managing his pain in superhuman fashion. Erik continued laying all his trust and effort down on the table as we crushed every obstacle that was presented to us.

Firing through that market on that final evening, we acknowledged the obstacles that tried to sabotage us and found ways to counterbalance them. Success requires you to amplify assets and compensate for liabilities, all the while looking for ways to be resourceful. At one juncture, as we were trying to make up ground on the leading team, I queried a young kid playing on a side street if he had seen any other "racers" run by. It was unclear if he spoke English, but he got the idea. I was trying to chase down some dudes that looked like us. He gave us the "follow me" wave and led us to a staircase leading up to an apartment. And there they were, the leading team, a trio of young, smart, athletic, and resourceful guys from California, the guys who were "supposed" to win the race. They had won the previous nine stages and were just about to solve the final riddle, scale a wall, and dance right into the winner's circle. We ran up beside them, surprising everyone but us. We solved that last challenge as quickly as we could. We scaled that final wall and rappelled down into the palatial courtyard that served as the finish line—five minutes behind the California Boys.

Second place.

Out of ten teams.

And although we still lost first place, we were pretty stoked. As competitive as the three of us are, we were absolutely thrilled and satisfied that in spite of Erik's blindness and Ike's ankle injury, we stuck together and represented ourselves proudly. We did the best we could, where we were, with what we had.

Landscapes change. The playing field is fluid and ever fluctuating. The only thing I have absolute, one-hundred percent control over is my attitude, and how I manifest the sudden changes to my well-thought-out plan. I believe our efforts in Morocco showcased what a positive outcome looks like when a team of individuals is able to acknowledge the adversity, maintain engagement through the process, and amplify those skills and abilities that are still intact and operating at a high frequency.

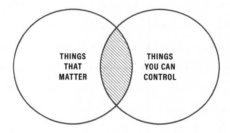

Our team had to reinvent our future once Ike busted his ankle. We didn't have a choice about his injury, but we did have a choice on how we reacted, and choice is the enemy of fear. We chose to embrace our situation and, in fact, allow it to bring us closer together as a team. We rallied around Ike's ankle and used it as a source of glorious intention.

Second place never felt so good.

Jeff and Erik charging through the Moroccan
market on Expedition Impossible.

Chapter 10: The VUCA of Corona

"Darkness, the truest darkness, is not the absence of light. It is the conviction that the light will never return. But the light always returns to show us things familiar. It shows us new possibilities and challenges us to pursue them."

— **Lois Lane, Justice League**

March 2020.

The human species headed into unquestionably the most VUCA development in several generations. It was real time and affecting everyone: young and old, rich and poor, conservative and liberal. Life as we knew it, was suddenly thrown into an absolute tailspin. If we were ever unclear what volatile, uncertain, complex, and ambiguous looked like, Covid-19 just showed us. As I write these words, we are still in the midst of quarantining, social distancing, and high acuity/high volume illness.

Every day presents a new set of norms and realities, much of it incomprehensible even a few months prior. If, in January of 2020, I would have told you that all schools, most businesses, and the NCAA Basketball Tournament (my personal tipping point) would be shuttered, you would have told me I was out of my tree, and that was just two months before it all became a stark reality. It is difficult to comprehend at this juncture how the events surrounding the pandemic will play out and how this episode will fundamentally change the nature of our global community, and how we interpret our human engagements. And also, just as importantly, how each of us decode and manage future VUCA events.

Although there was a high degree of volatility (in the markets and the economy), complexity (how the government attempted to provide financial aid; how the medical community worked to develop a test, treatment, and vaccine), as well as ambiguity (the opacity of how this would play out for our society in the long run), a large part of what we experienced with the coronavirus was based on **uncertainty**. Most of us were unclear as to how this thing was going to impact our health, our finances, our jobs, and our day-to-day social interactions. We heard mixed messages, at first:

"It's not that serious; go about your business."

"This is a profound illness that is killing thousands of people."

"Stay home."

"Go out."

"This thing is *only* affecting the elderly and immunocompromised."

"We have multiple cases of mid-thirties ER docs that are on ventilators in the ICU currently in the state of Colorado."

And two of the biggest questions: When will it end? When will life get back to "normal?"

This ambiguity leads to an overwhelming sense of fear and worry, based on uncertainty. But up until the Corona events, uncertainty has always held a special place in my heart. Those of us who have spent most of our lives seeking out adventure are drawn to uncertainty to a reasonable extent because adventure is defined by an uncertain outcome. However, the level of uncertainty that most of us experienced with the pandemic is not of that flavor. Seeking out an adventurous quest that is intentionally fraught with uncertainty is starkly contrasted with that of finding yourself with a loved one fighting for their life, or not having a job to return to after months of social distancing. For the purposes of learning from all the uneasiness associated with the pandemic, let's focus on harnessing and managing **uncertainty**.

Part of what drives feelings of anxiety is a lack of information. I recall sitting in a tent during a long and drawn out storm, way up high on a steep Alaskan mountain. While we chose a safe and protected camp, all around us huge avalanches peeled off the granite walls and reminded us that we were visitors here, only allowed to pass through if armed with sound judgment. I looked at the map for the umpteenth time, and my partner Joe simply stated, "If we weren't afraid, we chose the wrong mountain." But what about the uncontrollables? The length of time we would have to sit there was uncertain, and as a result, we were unsure if we had enough food, fuel, or toilet paper. Sound familiar? I was afraid. I was filled with anxiety because I was missing information and unable to conclusively predict and prepare for the future. I craved certainty to quell my anxiety, but that knowledge was elusive in the immediate moment.

When news of the virus first surfaced, there were many questions about the illness that it causes. The vast majority of folks hadn't even heard of it, much less knew anyone who had experienced this particular strain of flu. We understand the seasonal flu because we have firsthand, personal experience with it. That makes it less scary. Perhaps it was the effort to gain a little control that led to the panic purchasing of toilet paper as the first reporting of Corona started to hit our media outlets. There isn't any real practical reason to stock up on toilet paper, but it made people feel a bit more prepared for a situation rife with unknowns. And that is undoubtedly important because constant worry may make folks more susceptible to the very thing they fear. The more worried we are, the more vulnerable we are to issues like a pandemic disease. As silly as it may seem, having a huge supply of toilet paper may have reduced our fear and minimized the effects on our entire ecosystem. That, and washing our hands like a surgeon scrubbing in for the OR.

As humans we can read information, hear information from others, and take all that in, but personal experience makes a difference. Even as confirmed cases of the virus increased, the more that people learned, the better they felt. Once we filled in some of the blanks in regard to the mortality rate of the illness, whom it affected, and how it spread, we started to feel more secure. That knowledge became a disinfectant.

Unquestionably, humans generally dislike uncertainty, but some individuals have the ability to deal with it better than others. Numerous studies link high intolerance of uncertainty to anxiety and anxiety disorders, such as obsessive-compulsive disorder, depression, PTSD, alcohol abuse, and eating disorders.

It's important to realize that uncertainty is a feeling. Uncertainty is not a fact. It is not a tangible thing. Uncertainty is an emotion. We can easily become lost and overwhelmed in the current of uncertainty. By stepping back and learning to experience uncertainty as an emotion, we can be freed from the concrete feelings of fear and doubt that coincide with uncertainty. But after a lifetime of viewing uncertainty in a negative light, how do we rewire our brains? How do we acknowledge and externalize uncertainty in a positive manner?

When we enter a trauma in the Emergency Room, we always say, "The first pulse you should take is your own." That's always just a reminder to take a breath and go slow to go fast. This provides a calm and clarity that results in fewer errors. When those negative feelings of uncertainty creep in, try a centering activity like meditation, prayer, journaling, an unplugged face-to-face conversation, a run, a shower—anything to break the pattern and shift your thinking towards clarity and peace. In these moments, you can pause to view the circumstances in their entirety, determine the positive (versus negative) outcomes, and develop a better plan for dealing with the situation.

Yes, this takes practice—a lifetime of practice (and then some more). When you are paralyzed by fear or overwhelmed by the anxiety of the unknown, you are unable to experience the only aspect of life you can control: the present. Fully engaged individuals recognize that experiencing the present is the key to living and creating with intention. Practice engaging with uncertainty, acknowledging fear, and transitioning from preparation into action. And then practice it again. And again.

The most significant moments of our lives, the most important decisions, and the most meaningful choices are often characterized, in part, by uncertainty and fear. Take a minute to reflect on what it felt like when you went off to college or asked your spouse to marry you or started your first real job or had your first child. All are moments that will change your life as you know it, leading you down an exciting and unknown path. You don't know exactly how it will play out, and that can be extremely intimidating. But as Thomas Jefferson famously said, "With great risk comes great reward."

I'll never forget standing at the base of the Bastille, a prominent, 400-foot rock buttress perched near the entrance of Eldorado Canyon, just outside of Boulder, Colorado. It was a hot summer day; I was probably nineteen years old and so scared I think I may have quietly sharted myself. It was my first "lead" climb, and I was petrified. Lead climbing is when you are the first person on the rope, and, therefore, any fall ends up twice the distance from your last protection point. So, if you're three feet above your last piece of protection, you will fall six feet in addition to another foot of rope stretch. We call this being on the sharp end of the rope. You assume most of the risk and, therefore, most of the glory. It was the next progression for me as a young rock climber. My time had come to take the sharp end and all the fear and uncertainty that comes with it.

I inspected my rack of gear for the twenty-second time. I confirmed again that all the pieces of protection were all lined up on my harness in order of size so I could reach down and grab what I thought would be the right one, quickly and efficiently. My hands were damp with clammy sweat.

I had climbed this exact route several times before, as recently as the week before, but always as the second on the rope. This was different. Following someone else up the route was unquestionably safer, and the difference in the feeling associated with being on lead was going to be immeasurable. I took one final deep breath and stepped off from the dirt.

Why was I so scared? For sure, there was the concern that the impact I would make into the dirt from 200 feet up would leave more than a simple flesh wound. But the uncertainties that would lead to that impact were really at the root of the fear. I was questioning my own untested skill set. I was uncertain if the gear I placed in the rock would hold me in the case I fell. Maybe I was unsure that if I fell, my partner would catch my fall with the proper belaying technique. I was afraid of setting off on my own with just my technique to protect me. So, fundamentally, the uncertainty was my fear.

I slowly made my way up the rock, holding on too tight, breathing too rapidly, but moving, nonetheless. I placed a few pieces of protection in the crack of the rock, feeling marginally confident it would hold should I fall. Once I finally made it to the crux (the hardest section), I was dripping sweat and worn out from all the overdone exertion. It was time to place a piece of protection in the rock that would catch me should I fall on the hardest section of the climb—a fairly critical moment for sure. I evaluated the width and shape of the crack feature and then looked down at the gear that was hanging from my harness. Countless pieces hung there, shining in the sunlight, waiting for action. I pulled a piece off my harness and tried to slot it in the crack.

No go; too small. Then on to a bigger piece. No go; too big. All of this is taking place while I'm hanging by four fingers with my feet smeared to the polished rock wall. After a few tries with a spectrum of different-size equipment pieces, it became clear that with the overabundance of gear I brought along, I failed to bring the exact piece that I needed to protect the hardest part. I had no choice but to climb through it, with my last piece of protection ten feet below. You do the math on what that plummet would look like. Not pretty. So, this suddenly became "don't fall" territory. I nearly popped a blood vessel straining through the move, gripped out of my mind. But I got through it and to the top of the Bastille with a newfound appreciation for preparation, managing fear, and the unsung, all-time, world-champion variable—experience.

In my research for this book, I came across the teachings of a retired Navy SEAL named Pat Dossett. He eloquently related the mindset of a SEAL with the relevant methodology we can use to navigate ambiguous and trying times, i.e., the Covid-19 pandemic. He came up with three different strategies that he used in his military service that directly correlate to managing the uncertainties of everyday life that can leave us feeling overwhelmed.

First of all, Dossett points out that being overwhelmed is the consequence of trying to juggle too many mental operations at once, making it impossible to design or execute a good action plan. By reducing the set of operations, you relieve the load placed upon your frontal cortex (the region of your brain responsible for planning and action) and reduce the corresponding sense of panic. It isn't about how much you do, but that you focus on one specific task that you are certain you can complete. The challenge that once seemed impossible becomes doable by engaging in it piece-by-piece. The smaller the piece, the easier it is to accomplish and the faster your brain gets out of a state of being overwhelmed, restoring access to the brain circuits responsible for selecting and executing action plans generally.

A busy emergency room shift relies heavily on this premise. I am required to work quickly but not overlook a single detail or omit a single step, even when I'm responsible for five patients simultaneously. I have to remember to focus on one task I know I can accomplish in ten, or even five minutes, rather than dwell on what I need to accomplish over the entire shift. In the middle of the pandemic, there were countless issues that seemed overwhelming: trying to work at home and/or homeschool with your kids shaking the house to pieces, dealing with a spouse or parent who was in the throes of anxiety or perhaps the virus itself, the potential loss of employment and income, the uncertainty of how your bills would get paid, trying to save your small business, etc. I could go on and on. The struggles were countless for many and had to be dealt with for months on end. Whatever the case may be now and into the future, remember that the key to maintaining sanity and achieving success could be as easy as bringing your attention to one challenge at a time.

Secondly, Dossett recommends taking action when you feel powerless. As we touched on earlier, powerlessness stems from a lack of perceived control. Remember how the hormone dopamine is famous for its role in our sense of pleasure? Well, it also enhances our energy levels and sense of possibility. Dopamine is released not just as a reward for a job well done, but also by positive anticipation of rewards and completion of goals (see Chapter 1). When we freeze (which is the typical default when we feel a loss of control in a given moment), the release of dopamine is impeded, leading to an even greater sense of powerlessness. When you feel powerless, you must, instead, move forward. By taking action, you train your brain to repeatedly release dopamine, enhancing your energy levels, and creating an outsized effect on your thinking, mood, and ultimate sense of what you can control.

I live in Evergreen, Colorado, and it's called Evergreen for a reason. Our house is situated on two acres at 7,300 feet, surrounded by pine and spruce trees. Yes, it's beautiful, and it's our paradise, but it's also a tinderbox. It's not a matter of **if** our region will experience a massive forest fire; it's **when**. The fire risk is so high that many residents in our town find it difficult to obtain homeowner's insurance needed to replace their home if it were lost in a blaze. I have spent many nights lying awake, contemplating the fear and consequences of a devastating fire. Those nights leave me with a sense of helpless doom. I am keenly aware that I am unable to control whether a lightning strike or a neighbor kicks off a fire by tossing out a cigarette. But there are some factors that are within my control: attending local fire awareness meetings, mitigating the deadfall around my house, establishing a "water and soak" strategy for my property, and, finally, designing a hasty retreat plan for my family in the case a fire suddenly comes barreling down the meadow. I have learned to live in this wonderful place by replacing helplessness with action. By doing so, I have shifted my mindset from one of powerlessness to one of resolve.

One of the most challenging obstacles to achieving this mindset is to make peace with and not focus on those variables beyond my control. Feeling like you need all the information and possibilities (and their matching solutions) can leave you in a circular dilemma without end. I have found that by loosening my hold on a predetermined outcome helps me manage issues that are out of my control. Flexibility, grace, and being open to possibilities allows me to fully engage with the experience, and, in a sense, give it a life and vitality of its own.

Lastly, Dossett suggests that when we're in the midst of an uncertain situation and feeling alone, we should do our best to connect with our fellow humans/teammates. Feeling alone stems from the brain spending too much energy taking stock of our inner landscape. Linking with and supporting others rebalances the weight of attention we pay to our inner self and to the outer world. It also activates hardwired, ancient brain circuits that release those feel-good brain chemicals, oxytocin and serotonin and, at the same time, prevents the release of cortisol, which impairs immunity and promotes fear.

While practicing social distancing during the pandemic, those who lived alone or simply felt alone faced a time of extreme isolation. The restrictions that were put on all of us made it challenging to feel physically connected to others. I continue to be struck by the methods that we humans created and accessed during our time of quarantine to maintain a mental connection with others. All of the following allowed us to feel that critical connection to our fellow beings: watching videos of Spaniards do synchronized calisthenics in isolation from the decks of their apartments in Madrid; driving by our friend's house, alongside thirty other vehicles, to wish him a happy birthday; or partaking in my community's 8 p.m. howling session every night (yes, the hills echoed with howls every night), and we all felt connected in an unspeakable way. I am hopeful that after the pandemic has run its course, we can still maintain and value the connection we have with our fellow humans in a way that is lasting, reminding us to not lose touch with what is the most important: how we engage with our family members, friends, and neighbors.

The pandemic also highlighted the need to anticipate and plan for the unexpected. Many of us were caught flat-footed when Covid-19 hit

us, professionally, personally, and nationally. Professionally, many of us lost wages, were furloughed, or got sick and were unable to work. With unemployment claims cresting over thirteen percent in March of 2020, a large portion of our country had to consider methods that could keep them afloat financially as an unanticipated event derailed their normal earning potential. Business owners were faced with difficult decisions regarding how to cut expenses, whether to lay off employees, how to keep their business afloat in the changing landscape, or possibly even shuttering their doors indefinitely. Personally, those who didn't rush to the grocery store immediately and buy copious amounts of items may have found themselves running short on certain food, paper products, and/or medical supplies. On a national and global scale, the crises derailed not only healthcare systems, but also economies.

So how do you plan for an event that has very limited definitions and mysterious potential manifestations? It's like trying to map out the driving route to a particular destination (the town of Anticipated Triumph) and not having any idea which course can get you there. Where do we stop along the way to eat and get fuel? How many days will the entire journey take? The only way to effectively forecast for nebulous issues that could surface in the future is to use the historical markers that are at our disposal.

Although events like Corona are unprecedented and unique, we have other catastrophic events to study and lean on in our efforts to get ahead of the curve. Reflecting on and interpreting major events that took place days, years, decades, and even centuries ago allow us to forecast analogous events before they ever transpire. Previous pandemics give epidemiologists and healthcare professionals reference points, data, and strategies. Prior economic depressions are full of learning opportunities on how to prognosticate the next downslope and attempt to level it off.

Sometimes success is a result of taking actions that at the time may seem like overreactions. For instance, Japan and New Zealand closed all of their schools for a month with very few confirmed cases of the Coronavirus, and, at the time, it seemed slightly hysterical to those of us at the front end of the curve. Now, it turns out that they were pioneers in the social-distancing strategy, and it paid off with a rapidly decreasing spread chart. In retrospect, it became clear that shutdowns and social distancing were extremely effective and totally appropriate reactions.

On the home front, perhaps it's time to consider being some version of a "Prepper." Maybe not like the extremists that you encounter on those "end-of-days" docu-series on The Learning Channel, but likely a subtler version. Am I prepared to feed my family should grocery stores shutter? Do I have backup supplies on hand should there be another mad rush to stock our homes?

In many cases, the greatest mistake is the delay in taking action. One of the inhibitors is that, collectively, we are generally afraid of the consequences of error, and that restrains us from taking bold steps to intervene. When it comes to large-scale emergency management, perfection is the enemy of the good. The fear of failure as a result of bold action can be paralyzing. In many circumstances, having absolute confirmation before you move will result in missed opportunities. This does not mean we should jump into unclear, pending situations with complete reckless abandon. It simply reminds us to not allow the fear of failure to keep us from leading from the front. The tip of the spear is a frightening place to operate in, but without it, we are blunted and slow in our response times. In the case of the pandemic, speed superseded perfection. We witnessed how, when other countries handled their response by being fast and having no regrets, the result was more effective containment and a quicker return to their regularly scheduled programming. The balance here is not operating in a reflexive and hyper-dramatic way but, instead, to anticipate trouble, craft up a plan, and execute. This is generally applicable to many potential concerns that we all face on a day-to-day scale, both professionally and personally.

The reality is that the pandemic situation got harder before it got easier. The principles you leaned on then and in the subsequent days can have a tremendous influence on how you experience and emerge from times of turmoil. Just as with any challenging scenario, we have to continue to find learning points to store away for the next time we face unprecedented events, because we will. The fact that it's unprecedented means that it hadn't happened up to that point...not that it won't again.

By the time many of you are reading this, life will have returned to "normal" following the pandemic. We will have resumed typical day-to-day routines and wiped our brows from the beating we took. And perhaps after the dust settled, we realized how little we actually need, how very much we actually have, and the true value of actual human connection. I can only hope that we came out on the other end with a much deeper appreciation for our lives, for each other, and for the unrelenting truth of uncertainty. In that spirit, we will be better prepared for the next wave, which is an absolute.

"And the people stayed home. And read books, and listened, and rested, and exercised, and made art, and played games, and learned new ways of being, and were still. And listened more deeply. Some meditated, some prayed, some danced. Some met their shadows. And the people began to think differently. And the people healed. And, in the absence of people living in ignorant, dangerous, mindless, and heartless ways, the earth began to heal. And when the danger passed, and the people joined together again, they grieved their losses, and made new choices, and dreamed new images, and created new ways to live and heal the earth fully, as they had been healed."

— Kitty O'Meara

Epilogue

If I have learned anything from researching and writing this book, it is that life is hard. It is unquestionably difficult, fraught with challenges, disruptions, and tribulations. It always has been and always will be a tough road for all of us who are fortunate enough to live this life. Every conventional mainstream religion makes reference to the difficulty of life. Buddhist and Hindi texts both refer to the concept of Duhkha, which translates to the "suffering," "pain," "un-satisfactoriness," or "stress" of life. The Christian Bible refers to suffering in this life as preparation for heaven. The Torah and the Quran both teach about the indelible knowledge of discomfort and suffering. Undoubtedly, humans have experienced it since the first inklings of our species, and we have always felt it important to acknowledge and discuss the topic. The most profound question that comes with this knowledge is what we do with it and how do we manage it.

The Covid-19 pandemic was the most pronounced level of pain and suffering we, as a global community, will hopefully experience in our lifetimes. It forced all of us to step deep into the VUCA cave and have a thoughtful discussion on how we manage its subjective and objective meanings.

This life we live provides us countless opportunities to feel the opposing ends of the comfort/chaos gamut and everything in between. At times, perhaps it feels as though we have been spending too much time on the painful side of that spectrum. Other times, it feels like we are floating for a gratuitously extended period in the soft and easy zone. I suppose the sweet spot is to spend the majority of our time somewhere in the middle. In any case, most of the variables that contribute to where we presently fall in that continuum are out of our control. But what we do have absolute control over is how we react to all of the insults that come our way. The reaction to the action is what defines us.

That flight that just got canceled (you're not a six-month horseback journey from LA to New York) will get rescheduled. That computer that is painfully slow can be replaced. That car that just broke down can be repaired. That hot water heater that just crapped the bed…well, you get the picture. Each of these issues, at the time, appears to be an earth-shattering shitshow. But there is an immense difference between an inconvenience and a valid catastrophe. How we anticipate, manage, and execute these VUCA moments is what will define us.

So, let us go forward into this messy place, acknowledging that we, in fact, do live in a chaotic world. That much is true. The price of admission for this thing called life is that we are required to encounter volatility and uncertainty and complexity and ambiguity. And even though they are bothersome and painful at times, these VUCA moments are mandatory. They establish the paradigm for sorrow, joy, confusion, clarity, success, and failure. So, we take what the universe gives us, we do our best to manage it, and we find the opportunity to grow a more resilient and capable version of ourselves.

About the Author

For over twenty-five years, Jeff Evans' global experiences as a world-class mountaineer, guide, and emergency medicine physician assistant have placed him in some of the most chaotic and challenging situations imaginable. From guiding the first blind man to the summit of Mount Everest to being the medical trauma team lead for the Iraqi Special Operations as they fought to liberate Mosul from ISIS, Jeff has always sought out daunting and sometimes imminently dangerous projects.

He is the published author of *Mountain Vision: Lessons Beyond the Summit,* and is featured in the award-winning documentaries *Farther Than the Eye Can See, Blindsight,* and *High Ground.* He was the lead medic on the Travel Channel series, *Everest Air,* and secured a second-place finish with his team on the ABC adventure race series, *Expedition Impossible.* He continues to guide expeditions, volunteer as a physician assistant, speak to companies around the world, and seek out chaotic environments to work in.

Jeff received his undergraduate degree in anthropology from the University of Colorado in Boulder, and his masters as a Physician Assistant at Drexel University in Philadelphia. Jeff currently resides in Evergreen, Colorado, with his wife, Merry Beth, son, Jace, and dog, Roka.

To learn more about Jeff, check out his website: www.jeffbevans.com

To inquire about having Jeff as a keynote speaker at your next event, email: info@jeffbevans.com

  Follow Jeff on social media: @jeff_b_evans

Made in United States
Troutdale, OR
09/14/2023